Confessions From The Comments Section

Confessions From The Comments Section

THE SECRET LIVES OF INTERNET COMMENTERS AND OTHER POP CULTURE ZOMBIES

—◦◦◦—

written and illustrated by
Jonathan Kieran

Also by Jonathan Kieran
Rowan Blaize
The Hand of Djin Rummy
Rowan Blaize and the Starbane Exile

CONFESSIONS FROM THE COMMENTS SECTION: The Secret Lives of
Internet Commenters and Other Pop Culture Zombies

Brightbourne Media

Copyright 2015 by Jonathan Kieran

ISBN-13: 9780988568181
ISBN-10: 0988568187

Printed in the United States of America

This book is a work of parody. Any resemblance to real people, places, and internet
commentary is either intentionally coincidental or unintentionally coincidental (take
your pick) for purposes of optimum comedic and observationally witty effect. If one
happens to recognize one's self in any of these satirical and eminently humorous profiles, consider this a random but potentially quite beneficial experience on your long-
overdue journey toward self-understanding.

For Li'l Lloyd and The Big V

Contents

A Rather Forward Introduction

—⁓—

How far would you go, exactly?

What would you say to other human beings if you could go beyond the reasonable restrictions of social parameters, a sense of communal decency, established levels of acceptable civility, and the painfully incriminating awareness of your own soul-crippling insecurities?

How wanton and reckless would you become, if you knew you could get away with such liberties, all while entertaining an expectation of anonymity (real or imagined) and, perhaps, a naive assurance that you would never, ever be "found out" and forced to suffer the consequences—good or bad—of your giddy little expeditions into the wilds of human anarchy and chaos?

How far would you push the envelope? To the edge of the desk? Onto the floor? Or would you address that envelope with the tremulous hen-scratch of your existential discontent, lick the adhesive flap in a fluttering tongue-orgy of steaming saliva, seal it, stamp it, and shove it straight down the throat of the first person who has the misfortune of crossing your path?

"Special delivery, idiot!"

How bold would you be, in terms of communicating your such-as-it-is sense of wisdom or the darkest, most reprehensible impulses gestating in the cobwebbed and shadowy corridors of your derelict heart? If the mere guarantee of anonymity proved to be the grubby welcome-mat that transforms itself into a magic carpet, whisking you off to a realm where you could do things you'd normally consider uncharacteristic of yourself, then what might be said about the quality of your true "character" in the first place?

If anyone desires to know the answers to these questions in their own regard, and in the regard of millions of others, look no further than your friendly neighborhood internet comments section. Believe me: whether dangling at the murky bottom of an online news report about a local man whose trumpeting, uncontrollable flatulence has left him jobless, or serving as the coda to some ominous editorial lamenting the scourge of "micro-aggression" sweeping university quads across the globe, the average internet comments section REVEALS ALL.

The internet comments section has become the accidental cross-cultural polygraph of the human condition in all of its unfiltered self-righteousness and rancidity. The comments section is the perpetually doubling, bubbling, toiling (and troubling) cauldron in which the collective neuroses of the West are currently being stewed into a seething, apocalyptic jambalaya. Given that countless millions in the West are either fantasizing about becoming zombies or already conducting themselves like the aforementioned flesh-eaters, it must be a comfort to know that those feeling famished for a Gumbo of Ghoulish Gratification can always find the recipe, from start to finish, in just about any internet comments section these days. Indeed, comments sections are the roaring new Roman coliseums of our day; bread and circuses finally reborn from an abyss of centuries—centuries wherein the foul Muses of Fame-Hunger and Cyclopian Voyeurism struggled for breath in the aftermath of their catastrophic undoing, where a vile goddess muttered in the gloom, wondering if her doom-deadened eyes would ever again cast a baleful gaze upon the scattered remnants still clamoring for blood and humiliation and degradation.

Indeed, this Mistress of Opprobrium feared that her altars would never again steam and sizzle with the freshly spilled and scorched entrails of those innocent creatures sacrificed by slavering hordes that shrieked to the thundercloud skies, or rent their garments, wailing amid the echoes of forgotten caverns for Her baneful blessing. But she found a way to return, this multitasking Mistress of Filth and Fandango. Oh yes, my friends, She found a way. And what is her glorious, neo-Byzantine mantra, you ask?

"No! YOU'RE an idiot!"

The great writer, libertarian feminist and erstwhile Sibylline oracle of contemporary pop-culture, Camille Paglia, let slip during a 2015 interview with ReasonTV that she thinks the internet comments section represents "a whole new genre." She didn't elaborate upon that statement; it was more of a short, sweet grenade-drop in the midst of her usual rapid-fire commentary, but La Paglia loves internet comments sections, apparently. She is not alone, by any means. I don't think Camille has to worry about comments sections becoming a great new art form, much less a cyber-cornucopia limitless in its ability to proffer astounding expressions and staggering cultural revelations. Don't get me wrong; it is certainly possible to encounter these phenomena within this context, in an isolated way, but words and ideas, such as they are being employed by the comments section rank-and-file, are themselves already becoming outdated, replaced by the Lazy Brain's version of the increasingly passé and ever-so-twee texting emoticons—that glorious and illuminating Medium of Deep Human Interaction that we call: "The GIF".

If you don't know what a GIF is, you've either been off-the-grid, masticating beef jerky with a gun pointed toward the door of your underground bunker for the past twenty years, or else sequestered atop some goat-addled crag in Greece, reciting a string of prayers as long as the beard that snakes its gnarly way down to the hem of your holy smock. Whatever the scenario, you and the Modern World have essentially gotten together over coffee, had a little cry, talked about the good times, and decided to part ways for posterity, so The GIF means nothing to you, and it should probably stay that way, for everyone's sake. Denizens of any comments section, however, know all about The GIF. They are well-versed in the seductive sorcery that allows already-wan intellects to dispense with half-sentences, dangling participles and other egregious offenses against human language. They do this while employing reaction-shots of drunken TV "reality" stars, trick-performing terriers, lolling kittens, or prat-fallen news reporters who substitute for and speak the great volumes of wisdom that they themselves are otherwise presumably withholding for the later edification of their sure-to-be-captivated Special Snowflake children.

Returning to the aforementioned and intriguing glimpse of interest displayed by Prof. Paglia, however, I am not quite convinced that she was intimating an appreciation for the sociological value of comments section contributions, per se. Nah. I get the sense that she was remarking upon the explosive significance of internet comments sections as a cultural phenomenon in general, for better or for worse. I would like to imagine the great Camille perusing, for example, a typical comments thread at Breitbart or Jezebel and breaking out into the inevitable case of Contact Dermatitis of the Cerebrum that so many of us must endure following explorations of this nature. Indeed, it would appear that internet comments sections have skidded past the level of mere "phenomenon" and careened into the dour, utilitarian station-house of metaphor. There, they are lined-up, one platform after another, vehicles of doom languishing across a terminus of terror, beckoning wan passengers to board in a great, caterwauling, cacophonous parade of every untethered expression of human compulsion and degeneration imaginable.

.

Perhaps today's internet comments section may be likened to a looking-glass, one in which gibbering monkeys are driven by an insatiable curiosity to look upon themselves, only to rear back, so startled by their threatening reflections that they screech in horror at what they behold and proceed to hurl great, steaming handfuls of their own freshly squeezed feces at the glass, spattering and soiling the Mirror of Their Revelation until all sight of themselves is concealed by the salvific but scrofulous sheen of shit. Others probably fall, like Alice, straight through that looking-glass, entering a new dimension rife with bizarre and categorically irrational creatures.

Ah, but when the glass of this monstrous mirror is at last shattered and all that remains are a few perilous shards jutting from an empty frame, the contraption that is the comments section becomes a new portal entirely— a window upon the wider world, wherein the huddling masses are not confronted with the direct reflection of their own dark and devious selves, but where they can instead play the role of voyeurs, eavesdropping with obsessive devotion upon the constant vomit of unfiltered human bile that spews forth, much as the Romans once gaped and clamored from those coliseum seats for the satisfying sight of blood. Yes, even today, millions of hungry eyes watch for the slightest glimpse of crimson flow and nostrils sniff the air for a mere trace of the telltale scent, much the way sharks employ the *ampullae of lorenzini* … only in this case, humans seek to detect and then circle 'round the flopping, wounded fish of utter human humiliation before closing-in to stir up the froth of a good feeding frenzy.

In addition, for those members of the cyber-society whose stumpy baby-feet pedal with furious abandon astride cognitive cycles that still require the most foolproof training-wheels imaginable, it must be a daunting ride. I sometimes wonder what Camille Paglia would say, if I were to take her out for a beer and regale her senses with the kind of prophetic claptrap I am foisting upon You, Gracious Reader. Would she listen with a coy but wary interest to such ramblings? Would she excuse herself for a trip to the powder room and never return, leaving me in a puddle generated by the flop-sweat of my own embarrassment and a spilled glass of Dewars? Would she flat-out slap me? How would the conversation reach its *denouement?*

—⁓—

JONATHAN KIERAN: "Professor Paglia—may I call you Camille, or perhaps Messiah?—I want you to know what an honor this is to have you join me for a little drink and some light conversation. I must say, it was most unexpected to learn that you had accepted my clumsy invitation. Did you know that, if I were eating lunch *al fresco* at a chic bistro in the city, and you walked by wearing a toga and said, 'Come, leave those crab cakes and follow me!' that I would actually do it?"

CAMILLE PAGLIA: "No, I did not know that and, frankly, it means nothing to me. What I'd really like right now is for you to dispense with the cant and get to the point, okay?"

JONATHAN KIERAN: "Hmmm. A fascinating observation, Professor. I wonder … might you be implying that the dogmatic underpinnings of my overall theory would benefit from more philosophically denuded structural reinforcements?"

CAMILLE PAGLIA: "No. I'm saying that you need to get hold of yourself here, okay? I'm sensing a tendency to indulge in your own tangential appetite for existential rumination when the trajectory of your thought demands something far more linear."

JONATHAN KIERAN: "Would you at least give me a hug?"

CAMILLE PAGLIA: "Hell no. Go home and feed your cat if you need love. I've got a class to teach."

Man, that was a goosebump-worthy revelation, just to *imagine* the conversation. A veritable theophany. Whether that dialogue came to me as some sort of oracular vision, a direct telepathic communication from the mind of La Paglia to my own, or was merely a globule of coconut milk-fat from the magnificent curry I had last night pushing its way through a vein in my brain ... I'm not certain. But I'd like to imagine that, ultimately, La Paglia would be gentle with me, like Cintra Wilson, who is my other favorite ginsu knife-wielding scribe, and with whom I have actually worked and supped.

In fact, my experience with the legendary Wilson is a testament to the sheer power of internet comments sections, at least back in their primordial days, before the Jericho-sized walls of Western impulse-control came tumbling down and every Hun with a computer and a fart joke overran the Fallen City and stormed the Tower of Babel. I used to comment in such prolific, "notice me!" fashion on Wilson's popular *Dregublog* that the woman gave me a job as a featured columnist. Her reasoning may well have been, "If I don't, he's just going to smother my entire site like a particularly virulent strain of kudzu," but, hey, I took it. If you want to learn how to hone your craft, work with someone as brilliant and as certifiably scathing as Wilson, who also turned-out to be a crackerjack editor.

In all honesty, I never wanted to entangle myself with any comments section. I just wanted to be a saint, writing noble fairy stories that could possibly capture a stray synapse or two of interest on the part of young, innocent minds generations after I'm dead. Maybe I want to have my ashes placed in a magical platinum capsule and buried in a cave near San Luis Obispo awaiting the Fourth Age of the Eves (who'll know just what to do), but instead, here I am: shaking my fist and producing an indictment of a contemporary culture that seems hellbent upon lobotomizing the very precious minds I would one day like to influence with my tales of imaginary fluff.

7

Internet comments sections, indeed.

Why am I, a man who prides himself upon calm demeanor and the bearing of a zen-master crossed with some austere Catholic hermit dwelling atop a pillar in the middle of a desert, bothering to smite a culture that, by its very nature, is too consumed with its own noise to even listen to me, to heed my ululating warning? Is it due to sheer and excessive anger? I hope not, for I consider excessive anger a perversion, and it would send me straight to the grave if I thought for a moment that I was letting any sort of perversion get in the way of art.

Then again, after a good three or four minutes of self-scrutiny and forensic introspection, I realize that my perversions aren't anywhere near as perverse as the ones displayed by that vast ocean teeming with rancid, warped, and spiritually bankrupt cyber-dwellers. For this reason alone I shall have to keep reminding myself that this dubious book is not about me, Gracious Reader, it's about *you*, or at the very least about us, if one is going to simply press me on the issue until I'm practically ready to suffocate. And this book is only about you if you happen to recognize *yourself*, which I hope you'll do and commence to do us all a favor by getting yourself to therapy or perhaps to a particularly lofty bridge. Don't aim for the Golden Gate in San Francisco, however, as I hear they are installing the insidious equivalent of a gigantic butterfly net to ensure that all future pioneers of the Goodbye, Cruel World movement are thwarted, hindering these existential mavericks who are willing to spit heroically in the sneering face of life and leap outward (and then inexorably downward) into the waiting maw of Sweet Liberation.

Butterfly nets under the Golden Gate Bridge. Only Gestapo-hip San Franciscans would bumble so ironically.

Beyond all of this, if and when you read this book, Gracious Reader, and discover that your heart is indeed humorless, icy, and incapable of grasping the intricacies of satire, then catch a sympathetic air-kiss from the West before it freezes in the chill of your discontent, drops like a stone and finally shatters in glassy fragments at your triple sock-layered, corn-infested feet.

This book is about the twisted ways in which people reveal their true selves via Internet comments sections and social media interactions, all while thinking they are anonymous. That's it.

The book is structured as a series of handy profiles, if you will, with me describing each "type" of cyber-dweller, and what his or her endless, seething, writhing, self-loathing, narcissistic NOISE implies about what's *really* going on in their pathetic little worlds, and in the world at-large ... or the world "at-small." Moreover, given that the majority of prattle in to-day's comments section is not really "about the comments," but points instead to some deeper, ostensibly latent cultural revelation that is otherwise screaming at us in the face, I will have the opportunity to explore these fascinating corollaries and veer-off on a number of thrilling tangents.

I know. You can't wait to dive-in, but give me a few more minutes.

Despite being excited about the prospect of getting this book off my chest, I realize that there's a dreadful aspect to the process, as well. After all, with the act of turning one's laser-like sense of perception upon the complexities of the human condition (especially the more perverted aspects of that condition) there is a price to pay, a proverbial pound of flesh to surrender. You know what I'm talking about, Gracious Reader. Like you, I see what people do to each other and, often, I respond to this psychotic mash-up of vulgarity and sadism with wit—doubtless this shall be one of the reasons we'll get along famously, You and I. Nevertheless, before one gets to the "wit bit" at the rich, nougaty center of any epiphany, one just *might* have to process the disgust, umbrage, disdain, and, oh, yes, **all the things one will recognize about one's self** in the observation.

Comedy and satire are the dominion of people who are generally very easily bruised and who ought to be spending their lives hooked-up to a round-the-clock Grey Goose intravenous bag. But we want to make sense of the world's peccadilloes, too, and, in doing so, master our own character issues. Therefore, our brains and bodies react, and, once the switch is flipped, the whole Existential Crude Oil Refinery that clinks, clanks, and clunks within us begins to move: the conveyor belts churn into action; the gears start to groan and whine; the sprockets and dials commence to revolve.

And we turn it into FUNNY.

But you know (and I know that you know that I *know* that you know) that this sort of analysis has its cost. Looking deeply—even into the realms of the uniformly shallow—tends to demand its payment. While there is always a simmering, just-below-the-epidermis sense of *schadenfreude* at what I see transpiring in the world via internet comments sections, I discovered that it was quite therapeutic, summoning the powers required to get this particular book hatched and out of the Neurosis Nest.

Verily I say unto Ye: when you see a clown of any considerable caliber, spare a thought for the poor bastard. The interior of his or her skull is probably occupied by competing squirrel families locked in a constant flesh-shredding, fur-flying, teeth-gnashing battle over the pile of rotting acorns that fills the rest of their already cramped cranial cavity. Yes, this brand of summoning is an art form all by itself, and I clearly need a tranquilizer. You may need one, too, before the end. Maybe just a stiff drink. If that is the case, feel free to slake your thirst in the privacy of your own home or drop by my place, if you happen to be in the neighborhood. Cocktail hour can often start at noon.

It is also of paramount importance to assert that this book will be as much an honest reflection of myself as it will be about my thoughts concerning so many anonymous others. Hopefully, this statement goes a certain distance when it comes to answering the question: "How can a fellow who enjoys writing epic verse and pondering noble metaphysical mysteries *possibly* get-off on stirring the more fetid waters stagnating in the lagoon of Human Folly?"

(I know you framed the question in those exact terms, Gracious Reader.)

Well, therein lies my conundrum—or one of them—and likewise my salvation. I may do a lot of buffing and polishing of the pedestal upon which I try to position my Higher Self, but to let you in on a secret, I am also just a dirty little tadpole, like everybody else. May this be a comforting thought as you proceed.

If you are halfway-intelligent and possess even a shred of genuine cleverness, you'll probably like this book. It's going to be chock-a-block full of "our" sort of slice-em & dice-em gallows schtick. Then again, if you are a humorless dolt with an emaciated sense of wit, there is a good chance it will fly right over your inordinately thick skull. Too, if you are so self-consciously cerebral and transfixed by the individual trappings of your dilettantism that you are rendered unaware that being a dilettante is, in fact, an undesirable thing, then set your Umbrage Phaser on "stun" and zap yourself in the head. A little nap will be just the ticket. If you are excessively self-righteous, dogmatic about anything, or politically correct in that excessive, tiresomely pedestrian and sanctimonious manner we now see so often in the West, you may require smelling salts and the services of a Victorian era fainting couch. Or great heaving mouthfuls of detoxifying kale.

Otherwise, this book is intended for people who like to snicker a bit at the human condition, especially when screaming and clawing the walls has gotten them nowhere.

It is vital to document the existence of the pioneering minds in the following pages in order to preserve their deep and probative thoughts for the benefit of future generations and possibly even outer space entities. Extraterrestrials may wish to experience enlightenment at its very finest, a close encounter with brilliance and diplomacy, up at the sharp end, as it were. After all, there may come a day when comments sections are deemed, for the good of humanity and the sanity of civilization in general, to be a form of biohazard or metaphysical catastrophe. Thus, look upon this august and noble effort as a document of historical import and solemnity.

Therefore, in full hunker-down mode and drawing upon the Dark Powers this very moment, let us journey together. I am your Fellow Traveler, your Tour Guide of the Cyber-Cryptozoological Pantheon, shining a probative light upon creatures that thrive in the darkness and give up their secrets only as they squirm beneath the laser-like rays of our irresistible scrutiny.

In other words, until someone like Camille Paglia or Cintra Wilson looks into the matter, elucidates the issues, unravels the attendant Gordion-knots, and writes a doubtlessly superior book, you have mine.

An Amuse-Bouche of Angst Coupled with a Beguiling Soupçon of Troll (Just a Fancy Way of Saying "We'll Deal with the Trolls First")

—⚏—

I WANTED TO BEGIN THE book by tackling the issue of internet trolls head-on, because each one of the "types" profiled in this scholarly tome can indeed manifest itself, at any given juncture, in the trollish species. I have thought a number of things about trolls over the years. Yes, I have. For example, I always thought that internet trolls, the ones who truly drive us to the point of nail-biting distraction and force us to think terrible thoughts about the imminent possibilities of asteroid strikes, caldera volcano eruptions, population-decimating plagues, shark attacks when the Kardashians go swimming, etc. have besmirched their fantasy namesakes.

That's right. It is my conviction that *real* trolls get a bad rap due to their internet imitators and, being a fan of great fantasy novels, I think that this is a crime approaching blasphemous proportions. Sure, trolls in fantasy novels are, generally speaking, evil beasts with hearts of stone who feed upon the flesh of pixies and love nothing better than to suck the marrow from human shinbones at every possible opportunity, but there is a certain dignity to being a troll (or any kind of villain) in a classic or not-so-classic fantasy story. Take the late, great Terry Pratchett's trolls, for example. They were entities with some measure of resourcefulness, pride, and reputation, able to blend—well, not *seamlessly*, but reasonably— with wider societies (or at least in the big cities, like Ankh Morpork) and acquit themselves with the occasional hint of bonhomie.

Internet trolls of any and every variety, however, bring the fantasy species down. They drag decent, hardworking, marrow-sucking, skull-smashing, flesh-masticating trolls into the gutter, and I don't like it one bit. I suppose that the word "troll" does indeed apply when speaking of those who lurk in internet comments sections as if dangling beneath isolated stone bridges at foggy crossroads in moor-country, but it is my contention that the only similarity between the two types is to be found in the most cursory and superficial manner. The deal breaker, the repellent quality that soils the good name of the fantasy-story troll is, of course, the fact that internet trolls (so far as we know) are *human*.

This brings us to another enlightening tenet proven by scholarly study, rigorous scientific experimentation, and the conclusions drawn by any number of intellectual consortiums that have decided to consort since the beginning of Time:

Humanity can drag *anything* down. Even a whole genus of monsters.

I, on the other hand, always imagined, wistfully, for a much different type of internet troll—the kind of internet troll you might want to sit down and have lunch with at work or at a chic new bistro. Trolls that would redeem the entire image of their derided confreres in cyberspace. I fantasized about the notion, perhaps more than was necessary. Imagine Bob and Sheila, two hideous members of the troll species, exploring the first flutterings of new love at a swank little eatery in Trollville or maybe Noe Valley, getting to know each other over a light appetizer of human ears breaded in panko crust. Can't you just smell these nibbles, fried as they are to a crispy turn and served with a ramekin of spicy gallbladder aioli?

—⚊⚊

SHEILA: "This was a wonderful choice for our first date, Bob! I've been so busy at work, lately, and a night on the town is just what I needed."

15

BOB: "Glad you like the place, Sheila. Here, try some of this aioli. That little undertone of bile combined with the lemon zest gives it an extra piquancy, I think. Sets-off the cartilage perfectly. By the way, what line of work are you in?"

SHEILA: "I crawl through open windows at night and chew the fingers of newborn infants down to bloody stubs. Meh. It pays the bills. What do you do for a living?"

BOB: "I'm an anonymous internet commenter."

SHEILA: "WHAT?! Oh my God. That is *disgusting!* My mother warned me about men like you. You sick son-of-a-bitch. Waiter. WAITER! Bring us the check at once. This date is finished!"

—m—

The Smarts Vs. The Stupids

—◊—

Now THAT TROLLS ARE OUT of the way, let's get down to brass tacks, shall we? In North American popular culture, at least, the entire paradigm seems to be hanging by a rusty nail to a listing fencepost that boasts one warped and bullet-ridden sign. This sign reads: "TURN BACK WHILE YOU STILL CAN! BEYOND THIS POINT THERE BE IDIOTS." It's a bit sad to admit it, but we now live in a world wherein this colossal battle for attention and the acknowledged supremacy of one individual or group over and against another individual or group is, essentially, a war between The Smarts and The Stupids.

Before I continue, it behooves me to emphasize that I have no problem with the existence of this brand of differentiation, short of actual warfare, which always seems inevitable, anyway, regardless of brain-power. That being noted, I am not overly fond of Stupid People and have a sneaking suspicion that you, Gracious Reader, are likewise ill-disposed toward The Stupids. (Well, unless *you* are Stupid, in which case you'll have no idea that I am even referring to you, as you nod your over-calcified cranium with fervor, lamenting the existence of stupidity and therefore castigating your own species unawares.)

Looking at recent history, one is hard-pressed to pinpoint the exact conditions under which this enduring battle between The Smarts and The

Stupids experienced its genesis, but the nexus of the problem was most certainly archaic—Smart bacterium outmaneuvering Stupid bacterium in any number of primordial mud puddles, and so forth. Let the scientists continue to debate that pressing issue; my own observational capabilities leave me with little doubt that a radical shift has taken place in just the last twenty-five years, for God's sake:

Now *that*, my friends, was the proper, tried-and-true method of Stupid-shaming—a method that guaranteed you would start completing your homework lessons instead of wasting an evening crafting action-figures out of earwax and bellybutton lint. At the very least, this sort of wholesome humiliation would force you to hone your impromptu vomiting and/or epileptic seizure-skills in lieu of the next classroom quiz.

Today, however, the id-damaging, character-building scenarios of yore—those wonderfully painful experiences that all concerned parents and ambitious educators could rely upon to mold responsible human minds—have been obliterated (just like the dinosaurs) due to the globally catastrophic cultural impact of "geniuses" like Dr. Phil and Oprah Winfrey.

Yes, indeed: unconditional rewards pay-off, folks! Frankly, it strains credulity to imagine how anyone these days could possibly grow-up even *thinking* they are Stupid, which leads me to my next comment about the tragic magnitude of this problem. Ponder it with me. At one time, we were graced by the fact that a significant portion of the human population possessed a justifiable and healthy awareness of its Stupidity, and, inhibited by this helpful self-understanding, Stupid People tended to keep their mouths shut regarding matters far beyond their feeble cognitive skills. Remember those halcyon days? Remember the glorious *silence?*

Now, however, every person seems to be convinced that he or she is "reasonably intelligent" and the sociological ramifications of this egregious and pervasive misapprehension are most unseemly. Those who currently labor under this insidious delusion have changed the existential playing field, and not for the better I might add.

In any case, whatever Ultimate Solution one favors regarding The Stupids …

MERCIFUL = Let them live.
PRACTICAL = Sterilize them and their broods following a battery of FDA-Approved Stupidity Tests (Bell-Curve Negotiable)

… I like to have my Stupids clearly identified and demarcated in society, out where I can see them in broad daylight and where I can revel in the luxury of avoiding them for the sake of personal sanity and digestive comfort. Or, if wholly unavoidable, I like my Stupids out in the open where I can draw scathing attention to their Stupidity for purposes of abject humiliation and leisure-time jollies. In some ways, I am thankful for those foundational battles between The Smarts and The Stupids—grateful for the skirmishes that took place when we were still swinging by opposable thumbs amongst the tree branches. You know, back in the days before

God was stunned off His rocker to discover that we could do things like lust, pick fleas out of each other's pelts, eat fruit that looks appealing when we're famished, and, well, *die*.

Yes, it has always been grand to have a firm grip upon who falls into which camp when it comes to Smart and Stupid, hence the enduring popularity of this existential equivalent of a Shirts and Skins gym class team-selection. The mad rush to properly categorize everyone has reached a rather feverish pitch in our day, however, and it is dismaying to know that so many Stupids are clamoring for inclusion in the ranks of the Smart. You see it in comments elections all the time and one can hardly approve of such monkeyshines. Oh, The Stupids have always had little tricks and methods by which they have tried to breach the intellectual abyss that separates the rest of us from their dull ranks. They have looked-on in perplexity across this vast chasm, envious of The Smarts, who can gaze for hours with meditative expressions at their navels and mine one glistening gemstone of Truth after another. The Stupids, of course, wonder what all the fuss is about, unless there happens to be a fingertip's worth of sweat or perhaps an errant cookie-crumb that might be extracted from the afore-mentioned orifice.

Make no mistake: it seems that a great deal of this contemporary agitation stems from the constant truth that, if you are a Smart, you *know* you are a Smart beyond a shadow of doubt. If you are a Stupid, of course, you do *not* know that you are a Stupid, but all of the Smarts know that you are a Stupid, which makes the lack of awareness regarding your own Stupidity rather pointless. Frustratingly so. The under-appreciated upside to this whole conundrum is that Stupids never have to worry about whether or not they *might* be Stupid—The Smarts will let them know. Call it a form of pragmatic human altruism, a "service," if you will, and one that requires no recompense save perhaps a humble "Thank you" and some suitable acknowledgement of our superiority.

Now, some of you who think you are Smart are reading these words and a voice in the brain, like an insidious little worm masticating the center of a rotten apple, is saying:

In a word: YES.

If you are thinking those kinds of thoughts, you are probably a Stupid in swift need of re-categorization and/or reprogramming. You have been labeled incorrectly for ages, either by your Stupid self or perhaps by some other well-intentioned fool, like your mother, who passed the gene of Stupidity onto you in the first place. Maybe the errant label was placed upon you by a favored teacher who came across to you as devoted and encouraging for years. In your latent Stupidity, however, you mistook "devotion" and "encouragement" for what we ought to more properly call "Functional Alcoholism." You see, that beloved teacher was too weary from the drain of a failing liver to impress upon you the complex truth of your inferiority and thus found it easier to simply feign approval and pass you along to the world in your present state.

I am sorry that this happened to you, poor dear Stupid. Your injury may qualify as a tragic form of abuse meriting legal action with a mind toward the collection of retroactive punitive damages. Look into it. People are out there waiting to assist you.

Meanwhile, in the age of cyber-Intelligence, I have to admit it's becoming much easier for The Stupids to somehow camouflage themselves and scurry, crab-like, into the Smart Realms, without any of The Smarts knowing about it, at first. It is a most heinous deception that veritably cries out to the heavens for vengeance. Behold how the proliferation of helpful apps, Googling-as-substitute-for-thought-processes, and the scourge of anonymous internet plagiarism have each enabled a masquerade of monstrous proportions. Smarts across the beleaguered globe must act NOW if they wish to staunch this pestilential influx of Stupidity that threatens to dilute and forever intoxicate our synapse-snapping gene pool.

What is the answer, you ask? Well, If you don't know the answer, you are, demonstrably, one of The Stupid. That being noted, however, your status as a Stupid guarantees that you will never be able to comprehend a given answer, much less use it to any advantage, so I will reveal a few helpful hints for those unenviable Smarts who, due to circumstances beyond their control (workplace stress, spiteful offspring, Pinot Noir addictions, etc.) find themselves a bit slow on the uptake, at present.

Remember only this: The world is your sugar-bombed cereal box and actual human conversations, especially those that take place in internet comments sections, are today's Magic Decoder Rings when it comes to exposing the Stupid to a searing blaze of daylight certain to shrivel their writhing bodies like so many banana-slugs beneath a downpour of Morton's table salt. Examples can be found everywhere, revolving around any given subject. Online arguments over something as abstruse as the viability of shooting an aggressive dog can "evolve" into highly intellectual debates concerning the nature of pan-international relations, the inner-thoughts of African wildlife, and, of course, an Extinction Event. Behold the brilliance:

—␍␍—

EbenezerTaxi: Too bad if dogs die I don't care one bit about them. Who can live with these bastard wolves from hell that do no favors to a world of filth? They are dangerous noisy stupid and fucking beasts.

Bernadine: @EbenezerTaxi This dogs they are CREATURES ALIVE how could u think such is ok to kill dogs !!!! why your own kids are bastards too i bet! and you are the one who is VERY STUPID. Probably u are a Muslin 2 from far away and don't understand American.

EbenezerTaxi: @Bernadine Does the crocodile give two shits if the zebras are CREATURES ALIVE or not? No, so, what if i am?

Bernadine: LOL! So you admit to live with the zebras, u stupid Muslin.

EbenezerTaxi: No I dont admit it. And its Muslim not Muslin. Muslin is fabric you idiot.

Bernadine: Go for sex with the zebras BIGGER idiot.

ChantelMcGarrigle: It is the humans who need killing not dogs that suffer so many abuses on this lonely earth.

Danny6739: Man, I'm just waiting for the asteroid to hit and take everything out.

—◊—

Great Moments From Comments Section Pre-History!

The Garden-Variety Idiot

—⟋⟍—

As ANYONE WHO HAS SPENT any amount of time haunting the seedy back-alleys of an internet comments section knows, idiots and their derivatives abound.

Idiots on the web are ubiquitous—they are cyber-world's equivalent of those great herds of rambling, lowing, slightly cross-eyed and large-headed herbivores found loitering on some vast stretch of the Kalahari, bored out of their scrub-devouring brains, just hoping some Nervous Nellie in their midst will hear a twig snap or spot a lioness on the periphery. Then, to everyone's relief, the signal will be given for a thunderous stampede, which is a heck of a lot more fun than standing around chewing cud and looking stupid. As one lame-brained unit, they'll gallop away in a state of lathered, eardrum-splitting madness, vanishing into the colossal dust cloud of their own hair-triggered insanity, caught up in the drama, until they all rush into a river and plunge headlong into the current to drown or be dismembered by crocodiles.

It's fabulous.

Come to think of it, remember how great those nature programs used to be?Remember how television could enlighten a human brain, in the days before *National Geographic* and *Discovery Channel* and (Jesus wept) *The Learning Channel* started focusing less on the wildlife found in woodlands and jungles and deserts and started focusing almost exclusively upon specimens inhabiting trailer parks, storage facilities and pawn shops?

Those were good times.

Anyhow, if only internet comments section idiots were inclined to stampede away at the drop of a pin and throw themselves into the jaws of famished reptiles, we would all be the richer for it. But comments section idiots don't do that. They don't! They just hang around and masticate the same undigested clumps of slop they've regurgitated into their mouths a dozen times already.

———❦———

BB Riley: That's bullshit those stupid Californians won't go out there and hunt that Great White Shark that killed that poor guy visiting from Minnesota.

MandyPatinkin'sGoatee: @BB Riley The shark has a right to its territory. It was just doing what sharks do! The guy from Minnesota knew the risks when he went in the water.

BB Riley: @MandyPatinkin'sGoatee People have a right to go the beach and not get eaten up. They should kill all sharks that do this.

DenaSwayne: Who says people have the right to not get eaten if they go in the ocean?

BB Riley: @DenaSwayne God said so. In Genesis. Read it some time. We are to subdue the earth and its creatures. Yea, glory.

MandyPatinkin'sGoatee: Oh here we go LOL!

DenaSwayne: @BB Riley Sure, pal. Whatever. By the way the article said the man was probably targeted by the shark because he was obese and great white sharks are fond of anything that swims that's got a lot of fat on it. His own gluttony killed him. It was his fault. Not the sharks.

BB Riley: @DenaSwayne Your fat.

DenaSwayne: I'm not fat.

BB Riley: Then your kids are fat. And you live in California. Thats why your husband left you for another man.

DenaSwayne: My kids are not fat and my husband did not leave me for another man. You dont know nothing about me and my family.

BB Riley: I know that even a great white shark wouldn't eat your fat asses.

DenaSwayne: WE'RE NOT FAT!!!!!!!!!!!!!!

—∞—

Comments section idiots are indeed inescapable but, looking on the bright side of things, they are easy to identify. You'll never have trouble with species classification, if you decide to explore the panoramic diversity of any comments section ecosystem. Indeed, the Idiot will do you the favor of either readily identifying his or her idiocy via the rendering of idiotic statements, or else others in the thread will prove themselves most helpful by simply labeling the idiots, though this admittedly does lead to an inordinate amount of idiot-on-idiot invective. Make no mistake, however: the most common refrain ever to be found in the entire history of internet dialogue (and probably in conversations among aliens in other galaxies) is, without a doubt, "You're an idiot!"

Or it might be one of the numerous forms, responses, and incantatory variations of that potent declaration:

Your an idiot!
No, Your a idiot!
Yore a idiote!
Your mothers a idiot!
No, <u>YOUR</u> mother's a idiot!
LIE! Yore mother told me yore a idiot when she was in my bed last nite so <u>HA</u>!
Your a idiot <u>and</u> a moron.
Yorue an idiots idiot and morons moron, you IDIOT!

As one can see, the possibilities are, thankfully, not quite endless.

The only useful quality of the garden-variety internet comments section idiot is that, like the wildebeest or the gnu, the idiot is an easy target for those predators who enjoy stalking, torturing, confusing and ultimately toying-with stupid creatures. In this sense, idiots remind us of heart-tugging lessons best learned from iconic Disney musicals in which songs are sung against animated starlit skies about circles of life and so forth.

Basically, Mother Nature made things stupid so they could be eaten.

MIKE and MONA MIRACLE

—ɯɯ—

PREFERRED CYBER HABITAT: Glossolalia Chat!, Final Secret of Fatima Forums, etc.

MIKE AND MONA MIRACLE FORM part of the tragicomic Greek Chorus found in every internet comments section after a heart-rending disaster in which one or maybe two people survive (in at least a comatose state) but who were definitely maimed while everyone else was vaporized or dismembered. All of this, of course, was due to the amazing POWER OF GOD, who was apparently sleeping on the job to begin with or else the other 221 people in the crash would not have been annihilated.

There are reasons Mike and Mona think and believe this way, and their intentions may indeed be noble. We all desire to make some sort of sense out of inexplicable tragedy. But what Mike and Mona Miracle need to know is that every time they squeal "It's a miracle!" and believe that they are edifying themselves and others, what they are *really* doing is making God look like a complete and utter boob. Stop it, Mike and Mona, because the atheists have an iron-clad case against you when you do that, and I'm totally on *their* side in this regard ...

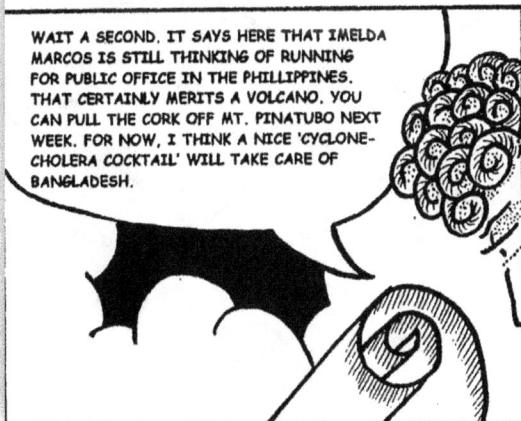

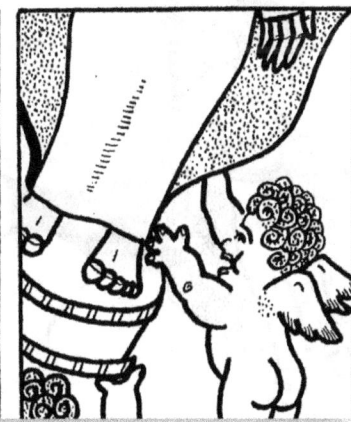

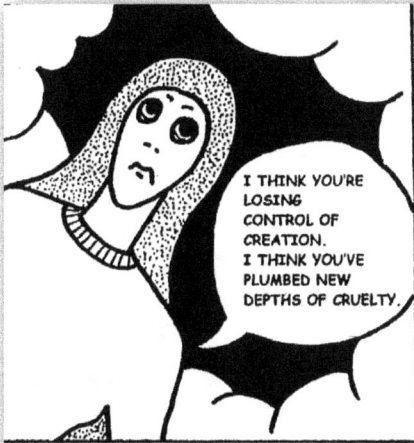

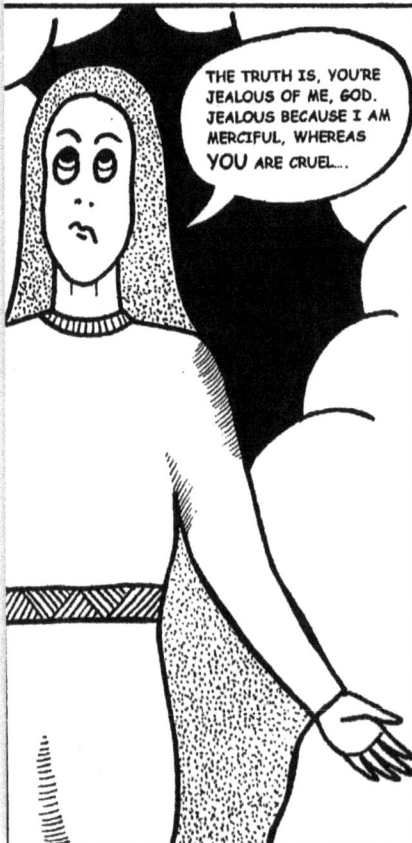

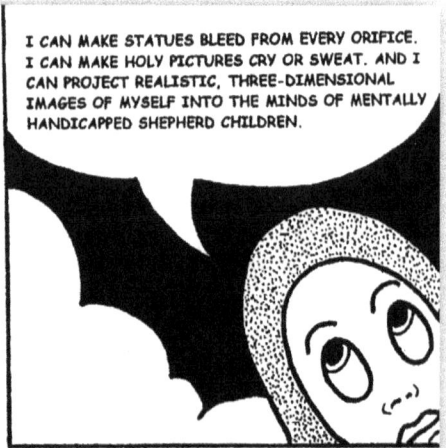

The Big Word Hurler

———⁂———

PREFERRED CYBER HAUNT: National Review Online

You know this commenter quite well. This is the person who is terribly insecure about his or her education and possessed of a heart as cold and black as obsidian kept in the freezer of some serial killer, right next to the pork chops. I am not maligning those who actually use "large words" in the course of normal conversations, within a context that reflects their typical brain-activity and the intellectual ambience of their preferred social circles in an authentic way. There's nothing wrong with using big words, per se. Hell, I use 'em all the time.

I'm talking about those who *use them in vain*, and usually without a clue as to their meaning and to the appropriateness of any given setting in which "big words" ought to be hurled. For example, this is my book. I have created the setting, and I'll write what the hell I want in exactly the way I wish to write the things I desire, in order to communicate. If you don't get the book, too bad for you. But if you went out for a couple (or a dozen) beers with me, I'd probably spend most of the time stuffing my face with french fries and wondering whether we should stay for the karaoke show and do some shots.

Right now, I'm talking about Big Word Hurling Fakety-Fake People. In internet comments sections.

It's a horrible combination—this insecurity about one's intelligence and how it stacks up against the intelligence of others. After all, as explained in the chapter on The Smarts and The Stupids, such insecurity is like the weapons-grade plutonium reactor that fuels virtually every neurosis in the Western culture. Festering insecurity about ... *something*. Imagine how bad it is for someone who doesn't at least have good looks to fall back upon! Imagine how trying it is for those who do not possess the kinds of superior attributes that allow sheer physical narcissism to override all attempts to bother with a pretense of intelligence! Imagine these things and tremble with a hypostatic union of horror and pity, O Gracious, Good-Looking Readers.

Don't judge me! I have great admiration for people so obsessed with their own beauty that they won't even take a stab at trying to come-off as Smart while using a ten dollar word just to impress someone like themselves. But the ugly and the physically repulsive who are *also* riddled with angst concerning their status as a member of The Smarts are among the most irritating denizens of any comments section, and they are among the most obvious.

Typically, a Big Word Hurler will show-up during the denouement of a very heated online discussion about, say, the merits or demerits of universal health care, initially dropping maybe one or two huge words as insults to establish their faux superiority over the others. Remember: it's imperative for a Big Word Besmircher to create an immediate and effective illusion of superiority in a comments section or else they'll get twisted in a knot of frustration and end-up kicking their cat in the head or putting some kind of spell on a stranger's latte at Starbucks later in the day, a spell that involves spidery hand-gestures, hissing in Sanskrit and a healthy glob of spit. Even so, the seasoned comments section observer should be able to identify and handle a Big Word Besmircher with ease because they tend to employ their Big Word of Choice in a manner that is either ludicrously out of context or altogether incorrect.

—ɱ—

NeedleNoze12: The propensity with which you directed your maladjustment at me reflects the abject lack of pestilential awareness currently recoiling in the sad case of worm-rot that is your brian. Moreover, your comparison of women's tennis with professional wrestling is ironic in the extreme.

BuckyWaits: What the hell? Your fucking crazy. Your six wafers short of a mass. Your two sandwiches short of a picnic.

—ɱ—

This sort of banter will go on for a few posts until some sentient commenter (be they Stupid or Smart) senses the Charade of Intellect that the Big Word Hurler is attempting to use as a cloaking device for the seething cesspit of his self-loathing, and goes in for the kill. Typically, this load of bullshit can be detected whenever someone peppers their online comments with use of the word "irony" or "ironic," which most of the literate world misuses in egregious ways and which even a well-funded artiste like Alanis Morissette managed to bungle back in the primordial mists of the 1990s. Trust me, when a Big Word Hurler resorts to playing the "ironic" card, check them for accuracy and potentially uncover a stultifying impostor. This is nature in action, folks—sometimes even better than a gnu-takedown by a pack of hyenas on the Serengeti. It can be just as riveting to watch … and sometimes just as messy. Entrails fly everywhere:

—ɱ—

Saraghina: Um … sorry, @NeedleNoze12, I'm not usually one who sides with a commenter like @BuckyWaits, but I have to say that you're completely full of shit. For example, you used, incorrectly and without a shred of contextual relevance, the words "propensity," "maladjustment," "pestilential," and "recoiling." BTW, the sad attempt to throw-in "ironic" really gave you away.

NeedleNoze12: @Saraghina As if a plebeian like you would ever encompass my superior facilities.

Saraghina: I think you meant to say, "As if an inferior like [me] would ever comprehend [your] superior faculties." Again, you used every big word in an almost comical and incorrect manner. Why don't you say what you mean, simply, instead of butchering thc English language and pretending that you are better than everyone else?

NeedleNoze12: @Saraghina SLUT!!!!!!!!!!!!!!! WHORE!!!!! WITCH!!!!!!!!!

—⌇—

As you can see, this kind of attack amps-up the bubbling cauldron of misdirected masochism in the Big Word Hurler until an eruption of Vesuvian proportions is unleashed. Only, in this case, it's the Big Word Hurler who generally ends-up covered in the suffocating pumice and pyrotechnic ash of his own, unmerited hubris. That's when you'll witness the breakdown. The full crack-up. The final death-kick of the gnu as its intestines are yanked in steaming coils from its ripped underside.

Magnificent.

Don't be alarmed by such shenanigans, Gracious Reader. Everyone in the comments section must feed, after all. Just take moments like this to hum a few bars of *The Circle of Life* and thank the Flying Spaghetti Monster that it wasn't *you*.

The Secretly Slutty Slut-Shamer

—∿—

PREFERRED CYBER HAUNT: Your sister's Facebook page after she's posted photos of a botched boob-job

IT IS DIFFICULT TO RECALL, exactly, which vortex of excessive PC sanctimony and manufactured fury swept onto the cultural landscape and set up a lemonade stand of ice-cold cultural taboo when it came to people not only expressing their disdain when others perpetrate what have been, for millennia, considered socially undesirable or counter-productive behaviors. But, man, has *that* tornado ever blasted a mile-wide path through the pop-culture pasture filled with grazing sheeple, churned them up into the air with the rest of the post-structuralist debris, then set them back down on the battered and bludgeoned game-board ... far more addled than they ever were before.

"BAAAHHHH! BAAAAH!! BAAAHHHHH!" say the sheeple, and the rest of the sensible world considered this bit of hogwash, thought about signing-up, and then decided to roll their eyes and dial-down the willy-nilly shaming without giving up that precious luxury and cherished pastime entirely.

Ah, the joy of shaming.

Seriously, think about it for a moment. Most people of good heart and in possession of even the slightest shred of linear thinking and analytical prowess are mortified when anyone shames another person excessively. Excessive shaming is tantamount to self-righteous judgment, and, outside the courtroom, wherein we all tend to agree that *some* sort of corrupt-if-orderly system needs to exist for the purposes of keeping the community safe from crimes of varying degrees of severity, we are not a people who like to be judged. After all, it is difficult to find someone worthy of casting stones.

I think it highly probable that all of us have done something shameful not only once in our lives, but possibly on several occasions—and over a period of quantifiable time that might even constitute a Bender of Shamefulness. Whether that activity involved way too much drinking, indiscriminate sleeping around, gluttonous stuffing of one's ravenous maw to the exclusion of proper childcare, video gaming while an infant's earlobes are being nibbled by rats in the crib and their streaming tears serve as water-slide theme parks for cockroaches ... shameful behavior is "out there." No matter how many people try to deny it, it's real, and it's rampant.

These days, a strange set of cyber-justice "warriors" love to decry the reprehensible tendency of imperfect individual humans to form a mob of bloodthirsty hypocrites. I'm totally on page with that, in theory. It's one thing to loathe those who salivate for the humiliation of one poor fool who got caught in the act of doing something everyone else has either done in secret or at least thought about with enough frequency to qualify them as Closet Perverts. It is quite another thing to banish the healthy, responsible act of social shaming from the human learning curve altogether.

Why?

Because, when the power of responsible shaming is removed from the equation of civilized development, we are faced with a world populated solely by Sociopathic Super-Slutty Special Snowflakes, and that is a world we *truly* want to avoid!

Yes, a pox, too, on the Magical Book-thumping prudes and puritanical chupacabras and their sour faces, glowering beneath pounds of shellacked Baptist-hair, eager to point a finger and spend every waking moment thinking of new people, places, and products to condemn outright. Away with their ilk, of course! Banish them to the margins! But hear me when I say that equally obnoxious and counter-productive to a balanced, sane society are the uber-PC Police haunting today's comments sections; these brain-trusts would have the entire notion of shame eradicated absolutely.

Without shame, we tend to unleash chaos into a muddied and waste-saturated mainstream entertainment culture already bloated with the consumption of hyper-sexualized, objectified mediocrity and the kind of sub-carnival sideshow voyeurism fixated upon the most base and vulgar expressions and emanations of human banality. Without even a side-helping of healthy shame, we create new grotesqueries masquerading and indeed infiltrating a spiraling society under the auspices of some giddy "Anything Goes" jamboree. The irony and the hypocrisy are staggering for the good of our collective Western sense of humor, as well, for in the clutches of such foolery, when either excessive shaming or excessive political correctness reigns supreme, the only stuff that can merit approval in mainstream comedy ends-up being fart jokes. When the cleverness and complexity of wit prove too much for the troglodyte Baptists to understand and too true for the supercilious PC-crowd to countenance, then all we're "left with" are the nosehair-curling realities of bodily emission and eructation.

DESTROY THEM ALL!

Yeah, that's probably not going to happen in anyone's wettest dream, but we all need to think about the consequences of these polarizing segments of society and remember that, in the very middle, up for grabs or for burning at the stake, is the Great American Slut.

"Who *is* the Great American Slut," you ask?

We are ALL sluts! Think about it. Just attach a few annoying buzzwords and trendy neologisms to a circle of Little People engaging in reality-TV pregnancy tests, dressed in prostitute garb while pulling each other's fake hair and scratching each other's faces in a chittering free-for-all and, *presto!* Such "entertainments" move directly from the margins of society to the center ring, resplendent under the klieg lights that flash "Acceptance!" and "Celebration of Differences!" and all of it proffered as comestibles in a main course fit for mass consumption at the All-Nite Buffet of Degraded Human Prurience.

What an insidious hall of mirrors, festooned with Bacchanalian pennants! Camille Paglia, who is usually optimistic even in the midst of her more cynical observations, was chillingly on-target when, in her 2015 interview for ReasonTV, she acknowledged her belief that Western society seemed to be in Late Phases.

Without shame, my friends, you must content yourselves with a culture leprous from the weeping pustules of Baby Girl Beauty Pageants, Obesity Gaining (or Draining) Competitions and a new set of everyday monsters far more terrifying and repulsive than anything James Cameron and Ridley Scott could have come up with. It is in times like these that I pine for the help of my Favorite (Presumed) Lesbian of All-Time: Lieutenant Vasquez, from the movie *Aliens*. Please, someone resurrect this bad-ass and magnificent woman and give her her own damned movie, already …

Some of us can only pray (or release our Calibrated Energy-Quasars or whatever-the-hell) and *hope* that Hollywood will bring back truly potent female action heroes to get jobs like this done.

Still, the fact of the matter is that it is truly reprehensible to isolate and target females for slut-laden invective while turning a collective blind eye to the high-fiving, rampant culture of "boys will be boys" and "notch as many on your belt as you can" notions. How about everyone staying *out* of the private sex lives of men *and* women? Let them all learn on their own, even if it takes numerous trips with sunken faces, sunglasses on, heads hanging, wrapped-in-a-trenchoat trips to the free clinic.

That'll sober-up sluts of every persuasion, one would think, and then there'll be no need for "shaming" … unless going to the free clinic becomes as routine as going to Safeway for groceries and you find yourself tripping over someone in a negligé to get to the frozen peas. By that time, all forms of shaming and political correctness are probably pointless. Besides, the loudest slut-shamers in today's comments sections are always the Secretly Sluttiest Of Them ALL! If one is masochistic enough to follow the thread of their incoherent ramblings, they always give themselves away before a moderator comes along and cauterizes the hemorrhage of insanity. The same goes for the Sanctimonious Shamers of Slut-Shamers!

I ask you: How hypocritical is *that* nonsense? As Cintra Wilson once emblazoned upon my poor brain: "Wheels within wheels, pal. Wheels with wheels."

The All-Caps Idiocy Maximizer

—✳—

IT'S BAD ENOUGH THAT THE Neanderthals dragging their knuckles through the steamy undergrowth of the jungle of Western culture feel an ever-increasing need to compete for attention by upping the decibel-level of their nerve-shredding, atom-splitting Howler Monkey shrieks, but aural irritation turns into visual dismay when this crass phenomenon is encountered online in comments sections courtesy of the All Caps Idiocy Maximizer.

Those of you whose ids were forever fused to your delicate egos by growing up in homes where walrus-like bellowing was the norm and screeching attained levels akin to a macaw being skewered alive up the ass with a rotisserie-spit have since gone in one of two directions. Either you've perpetuated the tradition of expressing yourselves like Alaskan wildlife or you've gone in the opposite direction and learned to not only appreciate the silence and the understated, but to cultivate its presence in your lives.

Of course, others among you simply cannot fight and win against the gene that prompted ancestral forebears to bray like donkeys, so you do the same when, for example, asking for an extra slice of salami on a deli sandwich. If lucky, however, you have learned to at least channel this perilous ability and turn it into something resembling a gift, a superpower. It can come in rather handy when on the verge of a bar fight with the odds stacked against you. One monstrous and unexpected mammoth-bellow can produce a significant shockwave, of sorts, stunning your foes into ar-rhythmia just long enough to let you make a run for it.

People who were not blessed with the Screaming Gene tend to learn it by example, these days, from any number of wig-pulling, face-slapping, hip-swaggering, epithet-hurling untreated psychotics being paid to display their "talents" on reality television programming. There's a definite cor-relation between these people and the All Caps Idiocy Maximizer, though I don't imagine any studies have ever needed to be done because it's pain-fully obvious, even to those who dedicate their lives to the obtainment of funds for the conduction of Painfully Obvious Studies.

Yes, it's quite simple.

People of less-than-fulsome cranial content see other cretins behaving deplorably in social settings on television, the corroded sprockets in the windmills of their desolate minds begin to creak a bit, and things like fake fame, fake beauty, fake reality, and fake outrage (desirable traits all, for The Stupids) are equated with being normal and—Alakazam!—You have a cultural plague on your hands.

The All Caps Idiocy maximizer is merely a comments section de-rivative of this phenomenon, a spin-off, if you will, of the moronic and inexhaustibly loudmouthed Accidents of Nature that haunt our exis-tence in the tangible, three-dimensional surround-sound world. The ways in which the All Caps Idiocy Maximizers unleash their foghorns of fury in comments sections are multifaceted, but their almost in-effable stupidity always features a common denominator. Trust me, it doesn't matter *what* the forum hordes might be blabbering about, because the All Caps Idiocy Maximizer will find a way to torture the eyeballs and accost the rationality of any and all participants by the mere locking of a button.

How empowered they must feel as they do it, as if a magical keypad talisman had been created just for them—a stab of sorcery for simpletons!

"Behold the button that will lift my ill-conceived, uninformed, sociopathic opinions above all the others, automatically rendering my head-thoughts as brilliant and as incandescent as a supernova illuminating some dark and dreary galaxy with the sheer magnitude of its fiery aura!"

Yeah. That's exactly what these clods think right before hitting the caps lock.

Even more befuddling, perhaps, is the eager queue of other commenters who fall over each other trying to tell the All Caps dingbat that he or she has "forgotten" to release the caps lock, as if it were some accidental, unfortunate oversight:

—∿—

Fistula21: PEOPLE NEED TO BELIEVE AND ACCEPT THE LORD JESUS AND ASK HIM INTO THERE HEARTS OR SUFFER THE BRIMSTONES OF ETERNAL DAMNATION WHERE THE SKIN WILL CRACKLE IN THE LAKE OF FIRE LIKE PORK RINDS BEING FRIED FOR THE CONSUMPTION OF DEVILS!!!!!!!

KneelyOHara: @Fistula21 Girl, you need to unlock the caps lock, honey. I already have a migraine and this aint cool.

Skibbereen: @Fistula21 Tone it down, man. Your caps lock is on!

MargaretCourtChampion: @Fistula I also believe in Jesus and that beautifully punishing Hellfire, but you locked your caps button and this will detract from your powerful message. Maranatha!

—⚉—

What are you all thinking, out there in Comments Section Land? Are you all drunk? Insane? These people *know* that their caps buttons are in lock and load mode. It's all part of the magic, the myth. All part of the complex mechanics of world-class strategy to be "heard." They know exactly what they're doing and you're only griping because you're jealous.

You only *wish* you had the good sense to maximize your own idiocy.

TOO LATE, FOOLS.

The Trendy Disbeliever Or: "I Know Why The Atheists Scream"

—∾—

ONE IS HESITANT TO SPEAK for any individual member of the new and trendy atheist brigade, but it seems a mistake for religious individuals and organizations of any color to dismiss their very real concerns and, indeed, their arguments. It is one thing for people of faith to countenance rude and condescending antagonism from atheists who plainly seek to humiliate believers and taunt them sheerly out of some vindictive desire for self-amusement and personal disdain. But those who antagonize strictly to belittle others come in all shapes and sizes, anyway, particularly when their tone reveals incontrovertible signs of ill-will and purposes far removed from reasonable dialogue.

Atheists in comments sections who care deeply about their convictions and who seek to discuss or debate others in predominantly religious conversations typically take the time and make the effort to frame their arguments and assertions respectfully and with coherence. Curiously poor grammar and obvious pseudo-intellectual mimicry doesn't *always* disqualify them from being worthy of participation in genuine discussion. Attitudes mean everything in this context, and atheists are too frequently and undeservedly attacked by religious zealots in comments sections, assaulted by "believers" who spew random Bible passages as if hoping to confound atheists. A Bible-thumper can sometimes be really funny in this regard, coming across like some half-baked sorceress hurling Scripture verses as if they were so many babbled incantations directed at her enemies:

"I rebuke you in the name of Hocus-Pocus 12:22!"
"I repel you by the power of Alakazam 6:15!"
"I abjure you by the words of Abracadabra 7:26!"
"I confront you in the spirit of Presto-Change-O 9:37!"

Seriously, that shit is ridiculous. Don't get me wrong: for an online atheist to sneer and to mock people of faith in a comments section is an exercise in futility and a demonstration of ill-formed intellect and immaturity. SIDE NOTE: I wonder if the Duggar parents say shit like: "Remember, children—There's always a "demon" in demonstration." Probably.

Nevertheless, our atheists deserve clear answers and churches need to get their heads out of their asses and give them some answers. They need to up their theological game and try to defend some of the basic doctrines that we all have come to realize are nothing but a load of horse-shit. I'm not talking about Christ Himself, or belief (via personal faith) that He might be the Logos incarnate. I have no problem with someone of faith that believes that. But when these buzzards try to defend this sort of belief solely from a hodgepodge of passages from a "book" that they seem to believe just floated down, fully-formed, from the blue, and which was written by God using the hands of eyewitnesses attached to holy puppet-strings, they need to get a clue.

Everyone with any sense or any desire to investigate objectively knows that the "Bible" is not some deified autobiography, much less an infallible one. It's the height of foolishness to use a bunch of so-called "proof texts" as a tool to convince a non-believer.

ATHEIST: "Why should I believe I'm going to hell because my head-thoughts are not exactly the same as your head-thoughts?"

THUMPER: "Because, look! It's written right here in John 3:16!"

ATHEIST: "But I don't accept your book as any kind of authentic authority."

THUMPER: "Then you'll burn in Hell!"

I really don't blame atheists and other skeptics. The jig is up for the Christian world, or at least that part of it in the West that attempts to confound reason, science and philosophy with the scribblings of a haphazard collection of antiquated myths, legends and proverbs. Maybe the avuncular Pope Francis should spend less time trying to convince the world that he's fit to pontificate from a background in Argentine economics, of all things, and more time trying to explain the FLUTTERING HOUSE OF CARDS that constitutes the foundational doctrines of his entire Church (and most of Protestantism, for that matter), largely due to some errant cogitations of the otherwise eloquent St. Augustine.

Indeed, a religious belief-system predicated upon the notion of inherent guilt and primordial culpability simply doesn't cut the rational mustard, anymore, and people are catching onto it, and they are reacting.

Yeah, you're damned right I know why the atheists scream, Clarice.

Think about what these Churches are attempting to foist upon people who are being exposed to empirical scientific evidence, these days. Are you really supposed to simply "believe" that there exists a being or team of beings "up there" recording every dirty thought you ever entertained in your head, inscribing it in a ledger? Are you really supposed to simply believe that, one day, after the end of the world, at the moment of cataclysm, billions and billions of souls will be held-up in some Judgment Line, like disgruntled shoppers behind the lady at the checkout who insists upon writing a check and bickering about whether or not her avocados are actually on sale. Are you really supposed to simply believe that you will personally "stand" (on ghost legs?) before an Almighty Being while He thunders from the Book of Life that you, Johnny B. Horton, on September twelfth, 2015, entertained invisible head-thoughts regarding the manner in which Mrs. Priddy in Homeroom looks when she soaps up her boobies?

Yes. The entire Universe and Time itself will STOP until these grave matters are weighed, judged, probed, parsed and settled before an audience of innumerable people eager to have their own filthy little earth-thoughts perused by the deity as angels look on, throwing eternal side-eyes. Or maybe they'll organize things efficiently, with different lines for different levels of perversion and random fantasizing, like Costco, just to get the crowds moving smoothly and quickly so folks can get through the Pearly Turnstiles and catch the A-Train to the New Jerusalem. I guess the unfortunate/unsaved will have to say their weeping, wailing, teeth-gnashing goodbyes before imminent pitchfork-impalement followed by a spectacular cannonball into the Lake O' Fire. That Lake O' Fire, when you think about it, is pretty amazing. Where exactly does that Lake get its Eternal Energy? Does it need to be serviced once a month? Does it need to have its filters checked? Is it periodically emptied for maintenance and upgrades? Is it sustainable? What is the effect of its carbon imprint?

Once again, I have great respect for those who possess faith in the deity of their choosing, because a faith that leaves room for Mystery and Things Unseen is a healthy faith. But I draw the line at literalists and fundamentalists and "proof-texters" who condemn based upon sources that are not even universally recognized as authoritative in any way, shape, or manner, and I understand the revulsion of atheists, even some of the rude ones. I also understand the trendiness of the "new atheism" as it has manifested itself not only in comments sections but across the pop-culture horizon.

A great deal of it was engendered by men like Richard Dawkins and Christopher Hitchens, the latter of whom is often referred to by his many acolytes and altar servers simply and affectionately as "Hitch."

Yeah. "Hitch." As if he were a chum, a pal, a lovable old schlub—just like Dave and Chuck and Fletch and The Beave.

As if Christopher Hitchens were the gosh-golly-gee shortstop on the softball team down at the neighborhood pub.

"Hey guys! It's Hitch! Hitch is here! Beers all around! Pull up a stool, Hitch, you gnarly old dog, you!"

As if "Hitch" would be the first to show up at your barbecue and you'd have to ruffle his hair and punch him playfully on the arm, because, gosh-darn it, Hitch brought only one six-pack to the shindig. That Hitch. What a kid!

I've certainly shared my thoughts about irritating Bible-Beaters, but you know what I wish? I wish atheists would "hitch" their wagons to a more viable guru than the late Christopher. They may refer to him in that bromancy, aw-shucks sort of way, but trust me when I say that Christopher Hitchens, a social butterfly who waved cigarettes like so many conductors' batons' and guzzled martinis at exclusive dilettante-salons across the globe and likely possessed his own gold-plated regurgitation-ewer would *not* be attending your beer & brats BBQ, or your pub potluck.

He would also not show-up at a local softball game unless he was guaranteed a private box along with a bevy of whirling fellators and fellatrixies, a fully catered caviar and foie gras bar, the golden-tipped vomit stick used by Henry VIII and an all-night Bombay Sapphire drip.

Not a single one of you happy go-lucky New Atheists would be able to get in the door of that party.

That being said, I do not cast aspersions upon the man's contributions due to the well-publicized and unapologetic features of his personal life-style. I think that those who point condescending fingers at Hitchens the Sybarite are perilously off-the-mark.

A brazen deficiency of admirable moral and ethical characteristics has never, de facto, precluded any man or woman from making valuable pronouncements or from engendering objectively new and sometimes brilliant perspectives. Still, regardless of his personal conduct and life, which I believe must be perforce excluded from any discussion of his cultural "value," Hitchens knew absolutely nothing substantial about the subject he so enthusiastically ridiculed in the form of a third-rate, opportunistic poseur.

His grasp of Western Christian theology, doctrine, orthodoxy and orthopraxy was staggeringly shallow—almost astounding in its cursory consideration. The man knew nothing, or next to nothing, about the complex and intricate belief systems that formed the infrastructure not only of institutions that do indeed deserve criticism of both the satirical and strictly academic varieties, but he knew nothing of the pedagogical aspects, cultural corollaries, with which the world's great religions have been and remain inextricably bound. He posed and sneered without even bothering to explore the crucial underpinnings of the very belief-systems he sought to discredit, simply by baring his yellowed fangs and casting a gin-blossom of infantile scorn upon random and excruciatingly obvious religious characters and characteristics. More often than not he failed to even grasp these things in any meaningful or persuasive way, except for those who were all too ready to sneer and to slaver, themselves, once they had found their impetuous pied piper.

Christopher Hitchens was intellectually slothful in his atheism. Today's atheists deserve better.

Look, I don't want to lose any sane and critically minded atheists, here. Truly, I do not. I am on your side in a multitude of ways. I share a great many of your concerns and, indeed, your incredulousness when it comes to the vagaries of organized religion and the fundamental understanding of the mere idea of a transcendent divinity, apart from the institutional framework, so bear with me.

I mean, if the big reveal in Heaven—the big satisfying payoff—is walking barefoot upon streets of gold and living in "many mansions," then isn't Oprah Winfrey going to be just a little underwhelmed when she gets there? I can see her confronting God right now:

"Nice try, Lord, but I had a bigger jade tub in Santa Barbara."

The Guy Who Reads His Bible On The Toilet

—⚭—

As some Gracious Readers may have already intuited, I simply cannot find enough excuses to slam and to excoriate fundamentalist/literalist forms of Western Christianity. If it were a choice between not eating for a week or bashing fundamentalists, I'd choose fundie-bashing every damn time. I'd choose it until I wasted away to nothing but ash, dust-bunnies, a clump of hair, and a couple of teeth that wouldn't even be carried off by vermin. Until there'd be nothing left of me to fry in that Lake of Eternal Fire created, staffed, and sustainably empowered by their supposedly Loving and Merciful God.

One of the great things that is said about Europeans (and especially Catholic Europeans, but I've met some awesome German Lutherans, too) is that they "wear their religion lightly" and I can attest to the truth of this. In general, Europeans don't seem to take their faith (or the institutional "Church") too seriously, but neither do they dismiss its value as, at the very least, an abiding presence that can sometimes help to bring little glimpses of the sacred into their everyday lives. They don't want religion coursing through their societies in brain-frying waves of radioactive judgment or preoccupation with dogma, but in subtle ways that allow them to experience the gentle brushstrokes of comfort, affirmation and stability that religion can impart … when it is not made the object of outright obsession.

This is an age-old and mighty tradition that helps good and average people invest the milestone moments of their lives—birth, baptism, coming-of-age, marriage, death—with a splash of ritualistic meaning that points to some greater, Unseen significance, whatever that Unseen significance may or may not be, ultimately.

Mystery. That's it. There's an appreciation of mystery in the "wear it lightly" European practice of hand-me-down pagan Catholicism, and it is palpable in the rank and file populations of places like France, Germany, and Italy, though maybe not in Spain. The Spanish don't seem to take anything lightly.

This phenomenon is refreshing to behold in the European spirit because it is edifying without being oppressive, celebratory without being sybaritic, and moderate without being anemic. Yes, the Italians, especially, in the heart of Roman Catholic Ground Zero, are a people who seem to revel in the pleasures of the Mediterranean lifestyle without being enslaved to anything beyond their straightforward passion for living, for existing in a world filled with many sorrows and hardships. But they are also aware, in an almost luminescent way, that the world is also rife with small and secret delights that never fail to charm the senses and steady the spirit. Italians wear their faith like clean summer linen and this is much to their everlasting credit, I hope. One has the feeling that Italians have done this even since the days before altars of Juno, Bacchus, and Isis were replaced by altars of Christ, Mary and the colorful parade of saints.

Lightly they wear their faith.

The same cannot be said for the Holy Harridans of Christian fundamentalism in America and elsewhere. These people not only do *not* wear their faith lightly, but, regardless of the denomination or sect or non-sect or sorta-sect, the American fundie spins the otherwise golden threads of their Gospel Truth into a tight-fitting Ensemble of Absolute Judgment and Condemnation and Goes to a Nightly Dance.

And they're trying to take over comments sections everywhere.

These are the creeping, mouth-frothing and baleful heralds of an apocalypse which they crave to see unleashed upon the world because, of course, it means that "they" will all be miraculously wafted upward into the clouds and made to stand in line for the First Judgment. Yeah. That's the judgment that comes before the Final Judgment, the one where those wonderful "Well-Done, My Faithful Servant" Crowns-O'-Glory shall be doled out, along with certifiably lamb's blood-washed white Salvation Smocks.

As a good friend of mine says so cathartically in times like this: "Fuck me runnin'!"

Meanwhile, on earth, those who never got around to saying the Magic Prayer will be prodded by demonic pitchforks down "below, below, below yo-ho!" but that's okay because the eternal and agonizing consumption of flesh in a fiery lake only highlights the fundamentalist's superiority. Heaven forbid (oops!) that anything interfere with the feeling of self-satisfaction and overall King James Version SMUG that these dear people need to experience in order to keep from doing all the vile and nasty things they always wanted to do … if not for the threat of jail or the eternal punishment of Sheol.

This, my friends, is true love. Expressed daily, and to harrowing perfection in Comments Sections everywhere, by the Guy Who Reads His Bible On The Toilet.

Kumbayuh Kathy

—⟋⟍—

DEAR KATHY IS THE ONE who always wants to make peace between the warring factions of coarse, crude, lewd, cretinous, juvenile, and prurient delinquents inhabiting a comments section at any given moment on the planet. Fortunately for Kumbayuh Kathy, those everyday comments section kerfuffles provide her with the opportunity to swoop-in like a Guardian Angel of the Insufferably Brainless and demonstrate her moral (and usually grammatical) superiority over people who are easily outmaneuvered.

Oh, there are priceless moments to be enjoyed by viewing internet comments sections, my friends. Priceless moments.

Let's face it, outclassing other people is really the whole point of Kumbayuh Kathy's existence. I mean, you won't see her trying to referee disputes between paleobotanists arguing over whether the Filincophyte was more appropriately confined to the Triassic or to the Jurassic Period. That stuff is out of KK's league.

Instead, like the old-time schoolmarm or that nasty lady in cat-glasses who used to sit in the front pews at church and look down her nose at the mothers who could not control their fidgety, hyperactive children, Kumbayuh Kathy comes into a comments section with a sudden and much-needed dose of handy tips about how everyone should get along.

Lord, if only people were a little bit more like her! If only they possessed her infinite wisdom, sense of diplomacy and perpetually imperturbable frame of mind.

—◊—

BerkelinaHathor: Everyone arguing here in this thread needs to just get over themselves and embrace the Oneness of Human Solidarity! Throw down your barbs, and zingers and hateful non-sequiturs! You are all fragmented, like smashed observatory windows on the Safari Tour of Life, whereas I, a humble seeker, have found the key to archetypal harmony, and am willing to share. You need to come together and find common ground, even as my uterus embeds itself in the hills of the vast green Forest of Equilibrium.

LeZoinks: @BerkelinaHathor We were just having a disagreement. You didn't have to shower us all with that self-righteous Earth Mama mumbo-jumbo. Some of us can handle the back-and-forth of a comments section without the need for a metaphysical referee. F*&k off!

FrauleinDotGoddard: Smell my sweaty lederhosen!

Virgil_theStagnant: @BerkelinaHathor Do you have a book out, by any chance? I'm interested in your theories.

—◊—

Of course, the fun part is watching Kumbayuh Kathy totally lose her shit and reveal her true self in a screeching paroxysm of ululating keyboard swamp-voodoo by the end of the thread. It doesn't always happen, because Kathy is a stalwart soul, but when it does it is like witnessing a supernova, or maybe some sort of tree-flattening Siberian Damnation Event, like the Tunguska Explosion. For the finer details of that sort of peculiarity, though, you would be advised to read the entry about Rhonda The Reasonable, who is not only Kathy Kumbayuh's first and most trusted cousin, but her dingier, darker pendant.

As I said before, Gracious Reader, there are priceless moments to be enjoyed on the internets. Scoop them up.

Priceless.

The 16 Year-Old Illiterate Literary Critic

—◊—

LET ME MAKE ONE THING clear: I am thrilled with the seemingly self-renewing energy resource that is comprised of today's ravenous, book-devouring kids. The enthusiasm for literature of all kinds demonstrated by teens and pre-teens is a most encouraging phenomenon in the midst of an otherwise digitally obsessed and hashtag-diminished culture. That being said, there's been a herd, a veritable mass mob, of new, self-appointed, teenage literary critics, as if the real ones—sequestered in New York offices and courted like ancient gold-hoarding conquerors that require appeasement at the walls of a threatened citadel—were not fucking vicious enough. Genuine, seasoned literary critics are very much like lesser deities lingering amid the crags at the foot of Olympus, demanding libation and ritual sacrifice before admitting access to the aeries where ambrosia flows into golden goblets like ichor through the veins of a smug coterie of Major Divinities lounging around the peaks.

And your chances of getting invited to the crag-parties are slim-to-none as it is. Forget about the peaks.

For a longtime writer, it's debilitating when a credentialed, pompous ass with a PhD and a thirty-year history at the *New York Times Book Review* slices and dices your novel as if it were a poisonous, bloated fugu fish requiring the sharpest and most painstakingly precise toxin-neutralizing maneuvers of a filet knife. Adding insult to injury, we now have platoons of teenage girls and boys attempting to render serious assessments of literature in the blogosphere and, after a broad sampling of their services, it pains me to reveal that—surprise!—most (but not all) of them are in way over their pay-grade, which is apparently nothing, so do the Existential Math on *that* equation.

It's an odd state of affairs. After all, an experienced writer can tell when a professional critic is bluffing his or her way through a book review when a deadline looms and the previous month has seen one cloudburst of migraines after another, soothed only by martinis and the consoling fantasy of suicide. But even a professional literary critic at his or her most uninvolved is light years ahead of sixteen year-old Katie Sniggenfester on her popular *I Will Crush Your Book Like A Bug* blog.

—⁓—

KATIE: "You know, I don't know about *Rise of the Vampire Sorceress* by new author J.C.R.L.T. Devlinson, because, it's like, she's, you know, trying to show me when she should be telling me, and telling me when she should be showing me, right? We all know what that means. And the plot holes are, wow, so, so, SO huge. Like, huge-huge. Plus, the vampire sorceress is kinda stupid, like, why would a vampire need to be a sorceress, and if she was such a great sorceress, then why couldn't she cast a spell and turn herself into only a sorceress and not a vampire + sorceress? All the other characters were awful, too, but I was having a rough week with my Mom's nagging, so maybe it was just me. But I don't think so. I actually threw this book at the wall halfway through reading it, so there's no way I'm going to recommend it. And I cried for an hour because I had to throw an actual book at something. <u>Not good</u>. I hope the next free book someone sends me to review is a lot better than this piece of crap."

—⟶Ⱳ⟵—

It is more than a trifle deflating when a truly proven, professional person in the creative arts feels obliged to court and curry the favor of a teenybopper with dismal grades in high school. Now don't jump down my throat. I'm *not* talking about the precocious and genuinely gifted teen book-bloggers. (You Know Who You Are.) I'm talking about the Katie Sniggenfesters. And if you're one of these types, I *know* your grades are lousy because some of these book-blogging kids are reading and "reviewing" a dozen books a week, with dozens more in the queue, ergo the nine kilotons of public school homework foisted upon them *isn't* getting done, or is being given the same desultory and unprofessional treatment rendered to the books they're supposedly analyzing. People who are in fact serious about perfecting their craft and who have years of demonstrable experience in working environments (wherein actual, bill-paying money is exchanged for a creative service) are not going to be excited about the prospect of finding themselves at the tender mercies of a sixteen year-old who is anything less than a recognized prodigy, or at least an undiscovered one.

Experienced creative professionals don't want to be encouraged to scramble for the attention of sixteen year-old book-bloggers as if they were so many dowager countesses and earls of renown, each holding the key to a potentially viral acceptance or rejection in the ever-expanding galaxy of pretenders who are apparently determining what passes for quality literature these days.

From whence did they come, these earnest little masticators of the written word who are now devoted to the yea-ing and nay-ing of works that should ostensibly be far beyond their malformed and still-gestating comprehensive skills and experiential capacities? Well, many of them seem to have been weaned on the same palpitation-inducing "glittery vampire-meets-sullen-gal" books that they presumably had to wrestle from the paws of their bored, Chardonnay swilling suburban mothers.

For heaven's sake, there are far too many starving professional critics in the New York and Los Angeles areas that ought to be more properly employed in the widespread discernment of lettered prowess, at least for all of the intellectual well-roundedness and incisive skill that the Katie Sniggnfesters of the world bring to the assessment of any single work. Katie's eating well. Her mom is cooking her three sumptuous squares a day, plus snacks. In New York and Los Angeles, people who studied for decades to become professional literary critics are opening cans of Purina in the cobwebbed shame-corners of expensive studio apartments. Alas, the critical bastions of our major literary cities arc now in danger of obsolescence. The LA Times, for example, is not even featuring a separate Book Review magazine any longer, and the Grey Lady in New York is thinning her ranks.

Thus, many of us are stuck with an army of book-bloggers and, to conclude the goddamned thought, it's easy to guess where many (though not all) of them came from.

Some kid discovered that the kiss of a brooding, perpetually adolescent nosferatu with boy-band hair and muscle-bound werewolf buddies makes for a nice little sigh into the pillow at night, when the outside world is nothing but a trip-wired Black Widow's web of stress, entangled with desperation and braided with stinging strands of expectation. We get it. We were all sixteen, once, and for many of us, books have always been a glorious escape. Enjoy them. But please learn to read them as children so that you'll absorb their virtues and carry their messages forward into some kind of functional adulthood before you reach the inevitable cliff of bitterness and plunge headfirst into a murky pool of your own pent-up disappointment and hostility. If you don't know what I mean by that, ask your mother, if you can rouse her from her afternoon Pinot Gris snooze on the living room sofa. She'll have plenty to slur about the matter.

Enjoy your books, kids. Blog about them with gusto. Tell your friends what you think. Share ideas. But don't try to make a career out of literary criticism at age sixteen because, chances are, unless you're Tavi fucking Gevinson-level talented, you won't be able to grasp the structure of a proper sentence until you are thirty.

Don't assume that the ability to turn on a laptop and create a webpage is tantamount to the kind of keen and probative universal insight that merits the clamoring of adult "writers" to send you review-copies of their work in order to elicit half-baked opinions. Have some humility. In case anyone hasn't noticed, teenagers—in most anything they do—tend to follow each other, sometimes mindlessly. Call them cliques. Call them packs. Call them demons. The point is: that's why they are teenagers. It's part of their genetic make-up. The book blogosphere, for many, is just an extended hallway with class bells ringing and locker doors slamming and all the little exclusive clubs going off in their separate groups, subgroups, micro-groups, and so forth.

There's nothing wrong and, in theory, everything right, when it comes to kids who want to blog about books. In fact, it's a glorious endeavor and ought to be encouraged with every fiber of a hopeful parent's or teacher's being. Bless them all, to the last. But don't pretend you know anything substantial about creative quality, Katie Sniggenfester, unless you happen to *be* that aforementioned genius. Trouble is, it seems as if every damn kid these days is being told he or she is a fucking genius.

News flash: IT IS A LIE.

Trust me, if you think your shit doesn't stink because you are a teenage book-blogger, that makes you just as spiritually moth-eaten and wicked as the blond cheerleader with the C-average and D-cup who called you a butterface the other day in homeroom. Of course, if you happen to be a male sixteen year-old illiterate book-blogger with a smarmy attitude, then that makes you as rotten as the dimwitted jock who pulled your shorts down on the basketball court in front of the whole gym last week. Fair enough?

I think so, even if you don't.

The Drunken Ranter Who Posts Drunk-Drivel Under His Real Name, Drunkenly

—⟊⟊⟊—

IN AN ERA WHERE ACCESS to the internets is as easy, affordable, and sometimes as necessary as is immediate access to all forms of refreshing alcoholic beverages, the phenomenon of Drunken Commenting represents an exciting new frontier in the reverberating World of Human Embarrassment. Drunken Commenting pushes new boundaries and expands bold, uncharted horizons when it comes to proving that things like good manners, temperance, impulse-control, and pausing to think before communicating potentially harmful or intense opinions are all outmoded relics of the past.

Just like shame! Or embarrassment itself, for that matter. Remember those obsolete and inconvenient socio-cultural annoyances? No, I didn't think you did.

Once upon a time, when people rode horses to work and Mrs. Olsen down at the mercantile (just miles from that Little House on the Prairie) had installed one of those Devil-Machines they called a "telephone," people only had to worry about the dangers of drunken-dialing. Well, truth be told, in Mrs. Olsen's case, she had to worry about drunken asking-the-switchboard-operator-in-Mankato-to-connect-her-with-that-smuggety-smug-Caroline-Ingalls-to-quibble-about-overpriced-eggs-damn-it-to-hell.

Things evolved swiftly after that.

For decades and maybe even generations, humans were forced to develop the nuances and possibilities of drunken-dialing when it came to delivering long-distance inebriated rants, though one supposes that more than a few cases of drunken-telegram-sending and even drunken-SOS-signaling must have occurred, too, birthing who knows *what* manner of destiny-altering trajectories. Otherwise, until fairly recent times, people had to be content with the drunken phone assaults.

Certainly, back in the good old days, if you lived far away from the person you had accosted with your blithering barrage of slurred words and stuttering tosspot insults, you might wake up the next day and, upon remembering certain things, crawl back under the covers and pray for the Angel of Death to just come out of the closet already and cleave you in half with his scythe. There was no way in heaven, on earth, or in hell that you were going to be able to "take back" that drunken phone call, so you might as well go straight into the Flames of Perdition and get it over with … or get it started.

Then, as the days wore on, if you did not die outright from shame and justifiable humiliation, the clawing fingers of self-recrimination would begin to loosen their grip around your conscience and you might even begin to convince yourself that things could be rectified with the aggrieved party, perhaps with a lovely Hallmark card:

> Your friendship I would hate to lose
> because my soul is hooked on booze.
> The drunken rant I spewed last week
> has left me quite ashamed and meek.
> And though this mess was half your fault
> let's bring our feuding to a halt.
> I shall forgive your selfish ways,

your viper tongue and drugged-out haze.
I'll overlook your rude remark,
your grating voice, your endless snark.
You drove me to the very brink
and made me reach for one more drink.
Yet all of this I will forget
if you'll accept my deep regret.
But should you opt to spurn my plea ...
... I'll liquor-up and call at Three.

Yeah, Hallmark needs to come-out with a line for *that* occasion.

In other situations, maybe a bouquet of flowers would do the trick, especially if it happened to be your Mom you so wickedly drunk-dialed. A new set of drill-bits or a subscription to Playboy might suffice if it had been your father (or your lesbian sister in Seattle) who suffered the stings of your hooch-hammered invective. The fact is, matters can be handled. Bridges can be rebuilt. Of course, you wouldn't actually call to apologize because no one in their right mind would take your call after the last fiasco. Still, there were options when it came to extending olive branches following an inebriated phone encounter.

However, when the Classical Era of drunk-dialing came to an end with the advent of email, the resultant paradigm shift simultaneously took the bottom out of the apologetic greetings-cards industry and heralded the complete disintegration of human shame. Why? Because drunken *emailing* paved the way for drunken texting and, later, for its most guilt-free and potentially destructive societal variant: drunken internet commenting.

You can really let loose in a comments section with impunity once you've had a few belts of whiskey and to hell with the repercussions! Being banned from a forum? Big deal! There are thousands upon thousands of comments sections to attack if you're not a particularly discriminating alcoholic jackass. Have you received a barrage of down-votes and flaming protests from your fellow commenters? Ha! Mission accomplished! That's the reaction you wanted in the first place. Resentful reactions are like music to your ears in this case. You're a drunk! In your own HOME! Anonymous to everyone except the NSA, the Illuminati, the Google gremlins and possibly a few bored Scientologists. If you are in the throes of a really sloppy drunk-commenting bender, you are a danger to no one but yourself, especially if you slip on the same area rug you wiped-out on the last time you went on a toot.

If you still possess even a modicum of shame and the conscience of a flea, you may feel a pang or two of guilt the next day and feverishly explore your history folder to see where you might have started any particularly bloody cyber-brawls. This practice is very much akin to the drunken sot of yore attempting to retrace his steps across all the previous night's strip-clubs, bars, and cheap motels to see where he might've misplaced his wedding ring before (or during) the blackout. But this sort of behavior, in the long run, does not bode well for posterity, my friends. It does not bode well at all.

You may be able to able to sober-up in a day or two, but let's face it: in the cyber-realm, drunken commenting lives forever.

Facebook: Curtains Wide-Open!

—◊—

THERE'S AN OLD STORY ABOUT one of the beautiful towns in coastal California very close to where I live. Pacific Grove is the name of the place and it bills itself as "America's Last Home Town" in a copycat or variant form of about 29,000 other small towns that sugarcoat themselves with a similar, syrupy dollop of quaintness. Pacific Grove is, in fact, a picturesque, seemingly sleepy little hub of charming dollhouse estates and streets flanked by broad sidewalks just itching to be promenaded-upon. You've also got your ramshackle cottages, staid churches, and antique malls. There's a healthy smattering of prissy local banks. Tons of mom & pop shops. Best of all, there are several lush public parks that sweep toward the ocean. There, happy seagulls glide upon thermals overlooking the broody blue of the glorious Monterey Bay.

Few of the town's ten thousand full-time residents, however, know that Pacific Grove got its start as a summer-camp for Christian religious fanatics.

That's right. Back in the 1800s, these were people who apparently wanted to isolate themselves (perhaps wisely) from the more sloven and perpetually tippling heathens living just a mile or so down the road along Cannery Row, the cheerful decadence of which was forever immortalized by John Steinbeck. To that end, there's an old legend about Pacific Grove that speaks of the manner in which its earliest settlers, at certain times of the day and night, were obliged to keep their household curtains wide-open so that the constables patrolling sainted local streets might be able to peer inside and verify that the occupants of any given cottage were not up to activities that might fall under the Begging-for-Hellfire category. A few folks "in the know" giggle about the old tale even today, but little do they realize that this phenomenon is still very much alive and well throughout today's society, particularly in America, and particularly among people of a fervent Calvinist Protestant persuasion ... or, as I am wont to describe them: Folks with Bibles in their Hands and Corncobs Up Their Asses.

Oh, stop judging me, already. YOU know as well as I do that there's nothing these so-called "Bible Christians" enjoy more in this world than keeping their household curtains yawning wide open for the prideful inspection of others. Those bastards keep the drapes far-flung to dash any and all doubts that fellow believers and heathen outsiders might entertain about possible family perversions and other sinful proclivities.

In the cyber world, however, these Bible-smoochers have a new-fangled and highly effective way to maintain such a triumphant facade. Namely, they do it with Facebook—the holy-rolling fishbowl of "I've Got Nothing To Hide" transparency in the new millennium!

Why Has Facebook Become So Popular With The Entire World, Much Less With The Bible-Thumpers?

I've done some serious research into this matter at various prestigious universities (Landover Baptist Institute of Creation Theory) and in a number of esteemed periodicals (Vogue, US Weekly, Cosmopolitan) and have reached a few solid conclusions based upon gathered data culled from the empirical evidence and so forth.

1. People are incorrigibly voyeuristic and Facebook allows the incorrigibly nosy to nose around the private lives of everyone they know and those they don't know.

2. People are incorrigible braggarts and Facebook allows incorrigible braggarts to make others feel inferior in terms of bank accounts, decorative skills, baking proficiency, the ability (or inability) to spawn attractive children, taste in clothing, and even the frequency of satisfying bowel movements.

3. People are famished/parched/starved for adoration, attention, and incessant flattery. Face it—most people are never going to be "famous" in the sense that talented and hard-working professionals like the Kardashians are "famous," i.e. people who have earned their fame via the sweat of their brows ("Hey! That wasn't *sweat* on her brow!" said You.) Moreover, most people are—I'm going out on a limb, here—probably never going to be royals, who were the precursors of the famous and who commanded vast nations of adoring subjects. But the miracle of Facebook allows every human being to cultivate an illusion of fame and royalty. It bestows upon the average user a genuine experience of absolute power, which, as we know, corrupts absolutely.

Yes, Facebook gives everyone a Magic Kingdom of their own. It's like Oprah Winfrey going bonkers on one of her old "surprise" giveaway shows, only better.

"And you get a fiefdom and you get a fiefdom and *YOU* get a fiefdom!"

4. Facebook allows average individuals to banish, exile, ostracize and essentially behead other individuals with the mere brush of an "Unfriend" or "Block" button. This is a most intoxicating benefit, indeed. After all, who in their right mind would pass-up the

opportunity to send someone into permanent exile? It's brilliant. The mere thought of wielding that kind of raw power and authority has ordinary men, women and children from San Diego to Samarkand drunk with desire.

5. Facebook allows an individual to get-to-know, keep-tabs-upon, and ultimately come to despise relatives they never even knew they had.

—⚶—

Nancy Delaine Worthington I noticed on my third cousin twice-removed Sheila's Facebook that she and her husband Daron are letting their 12 year-old, Sassy, wear make-up and big hoopty earrings along with these little leather miniskirts and it's all just so PRECIOUS! The rest of the family's been over to Sheila's page to have a look at the pictures and we all agree that some faces need a little extra help even before it's proper for young ladies to have the privilege of dressing like the occasional harlot. Of course I wouldn't let our Rebecca do that even if she looked like a hedgehog, but I'm not one to judge. I just want to be supportive and let everyone know I'm always praying on my knees every day for our wonderful Sheila, Daron, and Sassy. Of course, we only met them at the big family reunion last summer. I didn't even know they existed before that, but, my stars, how they have ENRICHED our lives! Praise the Lord!

—⚶—

6. Faceboook allows you to see how well your own high school pals and college buddies have aged and fared in life. Quite often, this awareness can increase one's serotonin levels to the point of Ineffable Bliss, especially if your old pals are generally fat, bald and reluctant to pluck the graying bristles from various facial growths. In this sense, Facebook is like a life-saving cyber-pharmaceutical, one that can be taken every hour on the hour, with no immediately

harmful physical side effects. Conversely, if *you* are the one who's fat, bald and unfamiliar with the power of tweezers, this approach can enhance those suicidal feelings you've been entertaining. No ever one said that the seductive allure of Facebook clairvoyance could not be twisted to unwholesome purposes. It's a double-edged sword.

7. Facebook allows employers to screen potential employees and anticipate potentially "ill-fitting" new hires ahead of time. This is the most valuable asset of them all, because unproductive or unhappy people in the workplace = Less Profit, and Less Profit = Corporate Executives Don't Get That Yacht in the Hamptons, and we all know that No Yacht in the Hamptons = The Arrival of the Four Horsemen of the Apocalypse.

—⚬—

Wayne Simkins the IVth I am so tired of going to one job interview after another and dancing like a goddamned puppet for these assholes in three-piece suits. I'm starting to get night-sweats. This morning the raisins in my cereal even turned into cockroaches and formed a chorus line to perform selections from *How To Succeed in Business Without Really Trying*. It was kind of entertaining, I admit, but I'm start to worry about my stress level. Anyhow, I have another interview this week with some guy named Upton MacGregor at Liberty Belle Insurance. I'll probably bring a pistol to that one, just to take the edge off.

—⚬—

The Special Snowflake

—⚬—

PREFERRED CYBER HAUNT: Grievances-R-Us, MySafeSpace.com and other hubs of incessant whining.

AT NUMEROUS JUNCTURES THROUGHOUT THE history and prehistory of hominid existence, it has probably not been a good idea to continually swath one's offspring in a cozy and elaborate cocoon spun from the well-intentioned conviction that relentless and unmerited praise (coupled with unconditional support) is the best way to prepare children for a life of success and fulfillment. No, not in a world that was clearly programmed from the start to favor the merciless, the competitive, the craftiest, the sneakiest, and the most selfishly opportunistic of cutthroat individuals, all the way from amoebas to runway models.

Many scientists have noted that natural selection has vouchsafed the birth of large-headed, clumsy, saucer-eyed and heartbreakingly helpless-looking offspring so that—particularly in the avian and mammalian worlds—even the hungriest and most stressed-out members of a species will be inclined to succor and nurture their biologically "cute" newborns, rather than eat, beat, or discard them. It bears mentioning that one can never entirely trust a Mother Pig on this count, as cute as piglets may be.

Statistics are evasive, but one gets the sense that this "attractive spawn" method works fairly well across the ecological spectrum, until we get to the primates, and especially to the human branch of that particular evolutionary tree. Then, all bets are off. Such complicated, boulder-brained beasts as "people" have produced a truly bewildering array of parenting methods from which to choose, especially in the past fifty years of the late 20th and early 21st centuries, in the West. This proliferation of often contradictory methods, along with the resultant legions of coddled children, is the sign of a gluttonous, corpulent, sedentary and habitually satiated society. This is a civilization that can take the time, even for several decades, to wallow and luxuriate in its outward conveniences and sense of communal safety.

Welcome, then, to prime conditions for the crystallization and subsequent celebration of the Special Snowflake Child.

Of course, we'd be wise to remember that, for the most part in the West—dismissing for the moment all relative distinctions between super-rich, rather-rich, fairly rich, rich, upper middle-class, middle-class, and low-income demographics,—most everyone is exposed to several regular forms of basic convenience that others in the world would describe as extravagances, as luxuries. Even the "poorest" in the West have opportunities to access things like running water, food, TV sets, video games, pornography and other basic necessities that a little family dwelling in a Mumbai drainage ditch would probably find quite commodious, in comparison.

Once a standard level of relative luxury has been established as actually existing, the rest is often (though certainly not always) a matter of who has more toys and more conveniences. The question of justice or parity or opportunity as a moral imperative will be put aside, at least for the duration of this happy little discussion. Suffice it to say that someone will always have more or less Crap than someone else. Everyone has Crap, but quantities of Crap tend to vary in the West.

Within this webwork we are faced with the aforementioned and wild array of parenting methods that, it must be stated, are not always commensurate with how much Crap people have.

These days, many bored and un-oppressed segments of parental society have the downtime to turn their geometrically acrobatic attention-spans to the plethora of ways in which they might overindulge their kids, ostensibly for the purpose of securing a child's future. Keep in mind that they also do it in order to make themselves look really hip and *au courant* in the process. I don't know where, exactly, the term "Special Snowflake" originated, or upon which deluded parent's lips the words were first uttered, but whatever its origin, we are now saddled with millions of "icy uniques" that, when gathered as one unified force, shall one day form a gargantuan Avalanche of Misguided Ineptitude—one that will sweep down from the dizzying heights whereupon their progenitors raised them (by helicopter) and suffocate what pithy remnant of staunch character remains in the sad, sad West.

I have begun to notice a great deal of bile reserved for Special Snowflakes, when said Snowflakes or the parents of said Wintry Wunderkinds show up in comments sections. Usually, the ensuing drama involves outright discussion about the way kids are being raised, now, and how kids are inclined to do or say things which are utterly obnoxious—something that seems to scream Entitlement. It could be within the context of a news piece about two ungrateful brats who inadvertently knock some old lady on her ass as she's leaving a grocery store. The kids were witnessed laughing as the old lady's hip began to crack in six places and she frantically grasped for her MedicAlert necklace. This sort of story, happening in almost every town in every county in every state in America, every day, like clockwork, brings out the Agitated Codgers, the Mike and Mona Miracle-types, maybe one Guy Who Reads His Bible On The Toilet, and anyone, basically, who might have a nostalgic yearning for the days when children were beaten within an inch of their lives for infractions against home and Heaven.

—⟋⟍—

MoistJudgment: The problem with kids today is that they ain't being knocked upside the head enough to teach them any responsibility! Fathers have no balls and they let the mothers fill their kids heads with all this crap about how "special" they are. My daddy used to leave welts the size & color of beets on my backside when I got smart and look at me. I ain't turned out so bad.

Dibley O'Ryan: Damn right @MoistJudgment! My sainted mother took a big wooden spoon to our heads until we had lumps like turnips on our skulls. We learned the value of a hard day's work at her knee. I weep to think of what she'd do if she were alive to see today's crop of self-absorbed brats. I expect she'd be swinging hammers in the streets and they'd have to lock her away.

—⟋⟍—

Met with such a barrage of resistance, this is when the Special Snowflakes and their advocates come drifting down from the frosty grey firmament in a burgeoning blizzard of bluster and blabber to defend their own ...

—⟋⟍—

Eryn Rigel Delicato: @MoistJudgment @Dibley O'Ryan It's because of such callous and cruel beatings that we are faced with today's uncaring, divided world, you two Neanderthals! Children are like precious rose petals, fragile and sensitive to the harsh conditions of an indifferent climate. They need devoted gardeners in order to one day shine the light of Peace for the entire Global Village to see and celebrate.

MoistJudgment: @Eryn Rigel Delicato What a load of shit! You must live in California, lady.

Eryn Rigel Delicato: Portland, Oregon, for your information.

Dibley O'Ryan: Holy Mother of God—even worse!

Eryn Rigel Delicato: Are you two telling me that you would beat your own children the way your blockheaded parents beat you?!

Dibley O'Ryan: Well, I would but I can't anymore. One of the cheeky little bastards turned me in to Child Protective Services and they came and my took my kids away last year.

MoistJudgment: @Dibley O'Ryan Don't feel so bad, brother. One of those liberal propagandists they call a "public school teacher" reported ME to the law when my Jeffrey whined about that overblown detached retina incident. I'm typing this comment from a correctional facility. It's recreation hour.

—⚬—

Now that I think about it, these new "Snowblower Parents" might be onto something, after all.

Only time will tell.

Unemployed Li'l Lloyd (W/ The Genuine Dream Job)

—ɯ—

PREFERRED CYBER HAUNT: National News Forums during or following events like Plane Crashes, Prison-Escapee Manhunts, Kidnappings, and Nuclear Meltdowns

DON'T EVER TRY TO DENY, fellow inhabitant of Planet Commentary, that you have not developed the skill to spot *this* frequent flyer in the Wind-Tunnel of Wasted Brain Cells. The internets and especially the comments sections are rife with these desperate creatures, and they fall into the general "self-proclaimed expert" category of delusion, tending to writhe out of the woodwork when there has been some high-profile disaster, or when a high-profile disaster appears tantalizingly imminent.

Has a harrowing plane crash occurred? Never fear. Here come not one but more than a dozen five-star, decorated pilots out of nowhere to offer the commenting peanut gallery their crucial analyses of exactly how and why the disaster took place, with minute-by-minute "reconstructions" that even the most unethical of the declining, attention-famished online news outlets won't venture to proffer in such premature fashion. The astute comments section observer, however, can spot these impostors with ease:

—ɯ—

DerrekSkyWings52: I piloted United Airlines jumbo jets for years before I retired with my beautiful blonde wife, Shelley, to our palatial ranch in Sedona. I mean really BIG jets. The biggest. And I can guarantee you ALL that this kind of crash would not have been caused by a sudden loss of cabin pressure but rather by a compromise in the fuselage directly related to the striation of the rivets. This might have been occasioned by any number of interfering factors, not limited to hand-held missile launchers, structural fatigue, and death-beams emanating from hostile extraterrestrial invaders. So don't believe the media speculation on this one, people. Trust an expert. I'll be in the forum all day if any of y'all have any questions.

—ɯ—

I mean, think about it. What are the chances that FIFTEEN international jumbo-jet pilots are all going to show up at the same time in one damned Fox News article thread devoted to a recent aviation disaster, each with his (or her) own convoluted and highly technical explanation of the tragedy, followed by a conspicuously vague recitation of "credentials"? Please. This is yet another inanity brought to you by the magic of internet anonymity: 26 year-old dudes who are under doctor's orders to rehab the carpal tunnel problem caused by incessant video-gaming pretend to be "fighter pilots" for a day, spewing a hodgepodge of half-baked speculations culled from a quick Google search of past disasters and/or the thoroughly baked Wikipedia theorists of those disasters. Doubt not, my friend, that we have become a civilization crawling with Googling, autodidactic dipsticks.

The same phenomenon applies to mysterious murders, disappearances, and terrifying medical anomalies that can be found in the news on any given day, and which are subsequently flogged to the point of oblivion in any given comments section. At times like this, comments sections throughout the obsessive, busy West are suddenly flooded with doctors, lawyers, private investigators, vulcanologists, archaeologists, theologians and even appellate court judges who have all taken time away from their highly successful and active careers to hover over their laptops, log-in to TMZ with monikers like "JUDGE American EagleEye," and expound to the uninformed with an array of revelatory minutiae intended to evoke exhalations of wonder and admiration. It so *great* to elicit these kinds of responses from people they can't see, and whom they'll never meet, and who'll never be able to prove that they are not who they claim to be. The same applies to those who use the anonymity of comments sections to somehow insert themselves into world events, however distasteful.

If comments sections tell us anything these days, it's that some humans have set the bar terrifyingly low (or is it high?) when it comes to soliciting applause as they gyrate like hobbled turkeys through the Limbo-Dance of Attention Deficit Affirmation.

—⟪—

Brenda DewBoys: I knew that hussy who snuck those chisels and drill bits and razor blades into those dirty convicts. They say she used a bag of frozen Bird's Eye Peas. I used to work with her down at the old abandoned shoelace factory and I can tell you she was just as big a slut then as she is to-day. She was partial to Bird's Eye peas then, too, and I know for a fact that she used to sneak spare parts from that aglet-machine to her boyfriends in return for favors of an unsavory nature.

Lottie K: Did she try to put the moves on your man, @Brenda DewBoys? Because she sure as hell tried to put the moves on mine, only she was working at the Pic-n-Save at that time.

Brenda DewBoys: She did in fact try, Lottie K, but I put the kee-bosh on THAT nonsense right quick. I went up to her at that aglet station and I says to her, I says, "Millie Stookey, you keep your grubby little pig-paws off my LeRoy. He may be a snaggletoothed ape with a hump that'd put Quasimodo to shame, but he is MY monstrosity. Go back to Ned the vending machine guy, for God's sake. You two were made for each other."

FXNutter: @BrendaDewBoys OMG! It must be so ironical that you actually knew this woman who has caused so much scandal around the world, and you actually worked with her. To have such an inside story like this is AMAZING.

Brenda DewBoys: @FXNutter Yes, it is ironical and it is also amazing. Believe me I lay awake every night trying to think if there was any way ten years ago that I might have been able to prevent this tragedy but as much as I lay awake I can't think of a thing, unless I had done what my impulses first told me to do and thrown acid in her face, which, of course, would have landed me in jail and then maybe you'd see me smuggling contraband to well-endowed jailbirds. But such is life. I chose the lawful path. There but for the grace of God, you know?

—꟫—

On the flip-side, Gracious Reader, I suppose it should inspire confidence in human destiny to know that, even in comments sections, there are still plenty of (well, let's say one or two) people who can see through such blatant ruses. Even so, in the dead of night, when the mind is working overtime and the synapses are firing, I have to wonder:

What is more terrifying? The fact that these people may actually *be* pilots, doctors, lawyers, and engineers and that all or most of them are demonstrably illiterate and/or mentally ill …

… or is it scarier that ordinary people in today's world are so famished for attention that, under the cover of anonymity, they'll concoct any lie they need to concoct—no matter how flamboyant and complicated—in order to *get* that attention?

Eh, I'm still wresting with the answer to that one. I'll let you know if I come to any resolution via a juicy Comments Section sequel, but *only* after I've finished getting my P.h.DEE in Existential Analytics from the University of Cair Paravel. It should only take three weeks to get *that* squared away. After all, I'm a shape-shifting surgeon moonlighting as a Supreme Court Justice for the CIA.

But Li'l Lloyd the Unemployed got his start somewhere. You know it.

THERE WILL ALWAYS BE POULTRY, BOBBIE JOE. DO YOU HEAR ME? **ALWAYS POULTRY!!!**

NOW GET YER FRANKS IN GEAR. THE DAY'S FIRST CUSTOMERS HAVE ARRIVED. IT'S THAT OBNOXIOUS LITTLE ELMER JONES AND HIS DISGUSTIN' FRIEND, LLOYD.

YOU ALWAYS PICK ON POOR LITTLE LLOYD MAGEE, LINDABELLE. DO YOU REALLY THINK HE'S LIKE THAT CUZ' OF SOMETHIN' IN THE WATER 'ROUND HERE?

NO, I THINK IT'S CUZ HIS MAMA AND DADDY HAPPEN TO BE BROTHER AND SISTER.

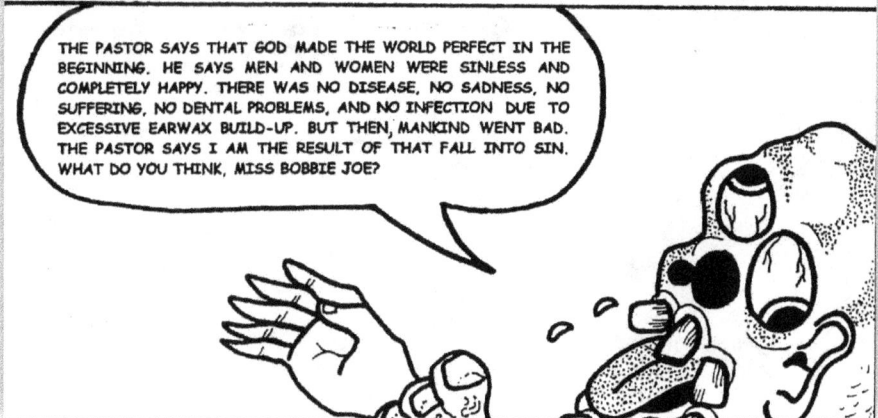

THAT'S RIGHT. AND I'M FIXIN' TO WIN THE WHOLE THING, TOO. HERE'S YOUR WEENIE SHAKE, DARLIN'.

BOBBIE JOE, YOU GOT ABOUT AS MUCH CHANCE OF WINNIN' RODEO QUEEN AS A FART IN A WHIRLWIND. THAT HONOR DEMANDS TALENT AND CLASS. YOU AIN'T GOT EITHER ONE.

OH YEAH? WELL I'M WORKIN' ON A REAL FINE SONG THAT I KNOW IS GONNA GUARANTEE MY VICTORY, LINDABELLE. I AM DETERMINED TO SNAG THIS YEAR'S DOAGIE TIARA.

BUT YOU CAN'T SING, BOBBIE JOE! I ONLY EVER HEARD YOU SCREECH THEM CONWAY TWITTY SONGS, AND THAT WAS 'NUFF TO CURL THE PUBIC HAIRS ON A POSSUM.

YOU'RE ALWAYS TRYIN' TO CUT ME DOWN, LINDBELLE. EVEN IN FRONT OF OUR CUSTOMERS. WELL, GO AHEAD AND MAKE FUN OF MY DREAM, BUT I'LL HAVE YOU KNOW THAT A MUSIC TEACHER DOWN IN PALATKA ONCE HEARD ME SING...

Celebrity Snarkist, Ph.d

—⚏—

PREFERRED CYBER HAUNT: Gawker, Jezebel, Dlisted, Perez Hilton, et al.

THIS MEMBER OF THE VAST cyber-Unwashed typically reveals himself or herself in comments sections that are well-established and which feature a cast of devoted "regulars" of all descriptions who have established something approaching a family unit. Comments sections with this sort of avid following are often difficult to "break into" because a kind of hierarchy or unspoken seniority pervades the atmosphere of uber-funk peculiar to that particular site. It's not that the usual suspects are by nature an unwelcoming bunch, it's just that they are highly suspicious of newcomers and transient types (presumed to be trolls) who want to engage in the sort of hit-and-run commentary that threatens the Family's established sense of security.

On commentary-driven sites like Gawker, Jezebel, DListed, and other pop-culture bastions, the commenters seem to comprise what outsiders might, at first glance, call a Comment Section Snark-Mafia. If you rub these people the wrong way, they have the cranial equipment to retaliate with all the vengeance of the most well-oiled, ammo-stocked crime syndicate. Only the wittiest will take their battery-acid infused expressions of caterwauling resentment to these kinds of haunts, and if they fail, the Family will close ranks and "go to the mattresses" if they must.

These people, who are usually and sometimes even delightfully clever (with more than a soupçon of schadenfreude) can make the Sopranos and the Corleones look like Quakers when it comes to eviscerating unwanted interlopers. If you tangle with them, honey, you had better have the power to fling barbs like a tarantula vibrates a cloud of urticating hairs from its abdomen into the eyes and nostrils of some blundering, hapless predator.

Celebrity critique sites attract some of the most clever and deliciously jaded commenters because one gets the sense that many of them are not only educated but also employed in concerns related, in one way or another, to the very industry that has turned their eyes the color of someone in desperate need of an immediate liver-intervention. Let's be honest: people who are urban, creative, associated with the entertainment world to a certain degree, and buzzed on Pinot Noir while still in their jammies at noon on their day off are interesting. The brain-thoughts of such people tend to be worth at least a cursory look, in my opinion. These are *my* kind of alcoholics.

One of the other great things about them is that you could wallpaper Buckingham Palace with the fucks these commenters *don't* give, and they are rarely hesitant to bring a tangy melange of Funny, Crazy, Fed-Up, Deadpan Goodness to a comments section in which the exploits of shallow, spoiled-brat celebrities are analyzed and harnessed to be transformed into existential fuel for radiant cynicism. These commenters achieve this in the way solar panels and wind-turbines convert the glorious elements into energy that might be used to power the very laptops utilized to slaughter vast herds of modern celebrities via relentless expressions of umbrage.

In the course of decades-long scientific research that required infiltrating and "getting to know" various species of commenters in this unique category, I discovered that my personal favorite was the Dlisted set. Dlisted's writers focus upon the lambasting of modern celebrity culture through the kind of wry, satirical lens that someone of my disposition could appreciate, with just the right amount of politically incorrect realism and no-nonsensical truth-telling. And they can occasional be quite gross, which only adds to the allure. The loyal commenters at Dlisted seemed uniformly sensible, with about 75% of the "regulars" displaying what I would consider consistent wit and a penchant for rational, if at times over-zealous, discussion.

—ᴖᴖ—

Jekkyl: That entire Hulk Hogan family strikes me as white trash. Was that racist?

Bananoromulus: I think the proper PC term is "Caucasian Refuse."

HurdyGurdyLaw: I'm at dinner right now laughing my ass off at that comment!

—ᴖᴖ—

Thank you, denizens of Dlisted, especially the demigod who apparently coined "Caucasian Refuse." These sorts of jaded angels are the kinds of jaded angels who deserve to earn a new set of wings every time they get an up-vote, but that's just my personal religious belief. I wouldn't want to impose my theological system upon anyone else.

As for the rest of the cyber world's less-incisive preoccupation with degraded Fame, are you surprised by the widespread banality of it all, Gracious Reader? You shouldn't be. So much of Western culture (especially in the United States) has devolved into a chattering, bread-and-circuses discourse about popular culture, with the declining Los Angeles entertainment vortex serving as an emblematic bellwether. But Hollywood is the same as it ever was, operating as some sort of *imago*-esque quintessence of the nation's self-fascination, derision, and the exploration of our collective warped consciousness. It is within this framework that people who possess the stomach and scimitar-sharp analytical skills to parse and probe the heights and depths of this phenomenon are bound to have the most pertinent, if not exactly enlightening, things to say.

As implied, the value of a commenter's contribution in such places is gauged by the number of "up votes" or "down votes" they receive from the rest of the Tribe. As it should be, great value is placed upon the ability to disembowel self-absorbed "famewhores" with the right mix of scathing humor, merciless invective, wry abandon, and a little thing that I like to call A Pinch of Self-Deprecating Transference of Judgmental Culpability.

This entire, fabulous recipe is, of course, activated with the indispens-able leaven of *bourgeois ennui*.

It's a heady and toxic brew. One can get easily swept-up in the churn-ing tide of snark or yanked blissfully out to sea by the undertow of chic disdain. I love these bastards, but had to withdraw from their esteemed midst when the time came to start writing this book and my email ac-count could no longer handle the notifications from Disqus. That being said, I must admit I have come to harbor an almost romantic affection for some of these tart-tongued tightrope walkers of the Cirque du Comments Section. I did feel, however, for the Combustible Lurkers who simply could no longer abide their wallflower status amongst the Celeb Snarkists, and who dared to dip a toe in the onrushing torrent with their own, sad attempts at repartee:

—⁓—

Matraca IceBerg: I've tried to get everyone's attention in this goddamn comments section for weeks!!!!! I have spent whole days and nights think-ing about witty quips to put forth about celebrities and famewhores and maybe grab one or two up-votes from people who feel maybe just a small flicker of charity in their souls, but NO! You sick bitches are JUST like the sociopathic monsters I had to deal with in high school. Mean! Bullies!!!! ASSHOLES!!! Now I'm leaving and going some place where my contribution will be appreciated. I'll have to shine my light over the heads of much stupider people at TMZ, yes, but it'll be a hell of a lot better than wasting-away here like a forgotten corpse in this whitewashed mausoleum of mirthlessness. (Hey — that's worth an up-vote, right? If someone up-votes me on mausoleum of mirthlessness I'll stay and do better. Promise!)

—⁂—

This, clearly, did not end well, and, after a bridge-burning combustion, the Elders closed ranks and proved themselves more than capable of driving-off the yelping hyena who foolishly entered the circle where all of the big cats were lounging after the satisfying kill, their paws and maws red with the blood of their latest conquest … or at least with the stains of Pinot Noir they had inadvertently spilled (out of "coffee mugs") all over themselves before napping at the keypads in their office cubicles.

Make no mistake about it: internet commenting up at the sharp-end is a weary row to hoe, my friends.

A weary row to hoe.

Hank, The "Closet-Repair" Specialist

—☰—

GOOD GOLLY, MISS MOLLY, BUT the closet-cases in comments sections do tend to give themselves away with far more flagrant idiocy than your run-of-the-mill Stupids. Threads of every sort are littered with these guys, whether the subject under discussion has anything to do with mancrushin', bromancin', or any of the multitude of contemporary buzzwords hanging like terrier-sized fruitbats from the lush foliage of the Homosexual Diversity Tree.

How do these Hanks give themselves away, you ask? Well, for starters, such corn-fed, truck-drivin', gal-lovin', Skoal-chewin', deer-shootin' dudes betray *way* too much knowledge about the guy-on-guy sexual practices they are going out of their way to repudiate and from which they are apparently dying to distance themselves:

—☰—

FlirtySanchez: These sonsabitches trying to make my church marry the gays are going to answer to THE LORD for this evil, the same way that Sodom and Gomorrah answered to it, with fire rainin' down from heaven and peoples wives turnin' into salt and such.

MothraWings: @FlirtySanchez Dude, NOBODY is asking your priests and pastors to marry same-sex couples, and I can't imagine many gay couples who would want to get married in one of your churches. You're making too much out of this, and I don't think we need to fight about it. I'm a liberal, but not ashamed to admit it. You're a Bible-believer and not ashamed, either, apparently. Let's just agree to disagree.

FlirtySanchez: @MothraWings What the hell kind of response was that bunch a words?

BoinkDexter36: LOL! @FlirtySanchez He's just mad cuz he ain't had his fudge packed while he puts his muscular, slightly hairy legs up over his boyfriend's perfectly tanned and gym-toned shoulders lately, I tell you what. Damned HOMO!

FlirtySanchez: @BoinkDexter36 HUH????

MothraWings: @BoinkDexter36 WTF?

—◊—

Whoa, dude, indeed! You have been seriously pondering these things when you take five minutes from changing the oil in your dying Bronco to type-out specific details and logistics (and you *know* these guys can only type with two fingers, so they're probably taking a good twenty minutes of their time to get these juicy details out there and shared. What does that little bit of info tell you?)

Reading an average comments section, these days, one could easily come to the conclusion that there are more gays in places like Tuscaloosa and Kalamazoo than statistics might indicate—and I'm talking about gays of the pathologically repressed variety. Spare a thought for these poor, lewd, rude individuals. Realize that the phenomenon of anonymous comments sections may offer the only chance these latent blockheads ever get to express the inner "phallus aficionado" that's just squealing to get out, and which has heretofore been psychologically buried to the point of near-suffocation in a swamp of Skoal-juice, Coors, and Aqua Velva.

Homophobia, like racism, is always going to be a blight upon the world of anonymous internet comments sections, and in some ways, as the powder keg of our culture swells to ACME Wile. E. Coyote "Explosive Proportions," it seems to be getting worse, rather than better. I don't care whether you're a triple head-bun snake-handling Pentecostal from the Ozarks or a New Haven Episcopalian maven with a mouth like a paper-cut: you ALL have a family member who is gay. All of you do. Shut up! Whether you know it or not (and you all know it, even if you don't admit it) you have someone close to you who is homosexual. A neighbor. A neighbor's neighbor. A friend. A cousin. A brother-in-law. A daughter. A son. Your spouse. And I guarantee you: *always* a fellow tax-payer.

Deal with it. No one is out to stomp on anyone else's hallowed traditions. Believe me—gay people are generally ingenious enough to adapt to the wider world while forming their own valuable traditions, if only because the need to be ingenious was forged in a constantly stoked fire of oppression, regardless of inherent talent.

If, however, you are at any time exposed to the sad irony of a Hank "Closet-Repair" Specialist in a comments section, have compassion, but allow yourself the little burst of satisfaction that comes from knowing that, for "Hank," it's all going to end in tears. Why? I'll tell you why. Because one day Becky-Lou is going to come home from the late shift at Denny's (her manager having given her the evening off due to the travails of early-onset emphysema) and she'll find Hank at home in the sack with Duane,—Becky's daytime lover—and the first thing Hank'll say is:

"Becky Lou, honey, this is *not* what it looks like. See, Duane here has had some back problems and, unbeknownst to you, I have been secretly practicin' to become a chiropractor. He was just helpin' me with my studies. Now, darlin', there's no need to point the rifle in this direction. Damn it, where's your oxygen tank, girl? You're imaginin' things, babe. Hallucinatin'! I swear you ain't *seein'* this, Sugar ... No, wait! Stop! Becky Lou. No! Beck———-"

Well, I guess we can only *hope* it all ends in nothing worse than tears.

The Kid Who Captured, Tortured
And Skinned Your Kitty

—◊◊◊—

HEAR YE, DEAR COMMENTERS AND contributors to the Great Cacaphony and all ye Donators of Doltish and Dilettante-*esque* Delirium to the realm of Incessant Babble … BEWARE!

By entering any given comments section you still risk far more than a likely encounter with forces as trivial and as harmless as stupidity, racism, homophobia, xenophobia, and the desire to perform the internet equivalent of some pervert in a trench-coat flashing unprepared strangers with a traumatizing glimpse of his withered and dangling unspeakables. Yes, these types can always be counted upon to sully the mind and further dilute the comments section gene-pool with their antics, but if you're not careful, you will also find yourself face to face with a genuine psycho.

This sort of encounter can be most troubling, and even dangerous, because these sorts often use the psychopath's renowned charisma and charm to engage the commenting crowd, carefully lulling those legions of gathered invisible people with no hobbies or productive outdoor interests into deep, sometimes meaningful conversations.

—◊◊◊—

CarcharadonMacarius: I see news about a mass-murder like the one in the article above us, and my goal is to unite all the broken and adrift segments of our damaged selves, bringing the most vulnerable and delicate members of our society together in one place, where sanity reigns and the sharing of pure emotions is not hindered. I'm just a single, self-employed, entrepreneurial Caucasian man, fighting through the shadows, but if I could reach out and reaffirm every lonely and frightened human being—man, woman, or child—I would give my last breath.

SueBeans: @CarcharadonMacarius OMG, that is such a beautiful sentiment. I'm actually weeping! Such a unifying moment. I glimpse a split-second of Light when I read comments like this one.

CarcharadonMacarius: Umm. Yes, you do, @SueBeans … and please feel free to send me a private message if you feel the need to dive deeper into your feelings and share the pain. I'm all about sharing the pain.

EsmeWwax: Why do any of us need *you* to encapsulate our grief, @CarcharadonMacarius? Your comment was almost as creepy as the article about these murders. @SueBeans don't trust this guy!

CarcharadonMacarius: @SueBeans, don't pay any attention to @EsmeWwax …   she is almost surely a bitter lesbian, and no one wants to ride that carousel. Follow your heart wherever it takes you.

SueBeans: I don't want to start a fight between commenters, but your empathy is the beacon I have been looking for, @CarcharadonMacarius.

EsmeWwax: Fine, @SueBeans, just be safe. But, @CarcharadonMacarius, if I ever stumble across you in real life, you had better hope you have your psycho-powers on Maximum, because I will reduce you to a pulp finer than the worst fiction EVAH.

—〰—

Then, with the stealth of a cheetah zeroing-in on the lathered, juicy hindquarters of some lethargic, feeble-minded herbivore that has become conspicuously separated from the rest of the herd, he will close-in for the chase, for the hunt … no doubt salivating at the prospect of consuming the ultimate prize.

Unless he meets EsmeWwax.

What can I say? Folks of the Drunken Persuasion tend to find themselves in this sort of online predicament when they let the ole guard down, with comments section conversations ending in a totally unexpected psycho-query:

CarchardonMacarius: "So, @SueBeans, you want 2 mayB come over and see the collection of kittens I skinned in the neighborhood this week?"

And, in the horror and shock of this revelation, amid the terror and petrifying grip of your own, bloodcurdling fear, you (like SueBeans) are too drunk to remember that you already gave the crazy bastard your phone number and home address an hour ago.

But that's okay. It's only an internet comments section.

This nut is probably in Seattle. You're in Orlando.

Wait a second, what's that noise?

Oh. It's just your cell phone, ringing. Better go find it. You left it downstairs in the kitchen. In the dark.

Where the knives are.

The Gleeful Racist

—〰—

SOME OF THE THINGS I have seen written anonymously about various races of people, without provocation, without instigation, make the veins crave an antifreeze I.V. There are many willful stupidities of which the human mind is capable, but abject racism appears, in some respects, to be the most horrendous of them all.

These paragons of Blackhearted Malignancy scarcely require an introduction and merit description perhaps even less than that, but comments sections are fairly infested with them, these days, which begs the question: From whence do they come and whither do they go?

Sadly, the answer to this question is: Everywhere. They come from every walk of life, economic level, city, state, town, and hamlet. There shall never be a lack, I fear, of those willing and able to suppress any shred of reason and sensibility that might flicker in the loathsome darkness of their cavernous souls. They prefer instead instead to allow the chilly zephyrs of wickedness to howl through the empty, desiccated husks of a strangled collective consciousness, empowering them to despise other human beings first, foremost, and forever … solely due to the color of their skin, the land of their birth, or the sheer physicality within which a person's being happens to be ensconced.

Worse, they perpetrate this shit gleefully.

Yes, there may be degrees of severity and culpability when it comes to the spirit that willfully harbors racism—miseducation, miscegenation, mental illness and flat-out cold-blooded stupidity may be mitigating factors—but nothing occludes the piercing rays of radioactive evil that spread the devastation of true racism like a rampant and burgeoning cancer through even one human individual's existence, and, to the despair of decent people, through entire societies.

One is tempted to laugh at them, to ridicule them as a means of reclaiming some sense of dignity and waging some tangible form of war against such insurmountable hatred. But, no, the Gleeful Racist isn't even worthy of satire.

Some evils are perhaps too dark to be mocked.

Rather, I suggest that Gleeful Racists should all be shunned until, by some happy chance, the world of humanity has evolved to the point wherein such thinking is extinct or impossible.

But don't hold your breath on that count.

There is no opposite side to the filthy, corroded coin of racism, save for unconditional tolerance of everyone and anyone and anything at all times and in all situations, and the only person on earth capable of *that* sort of divine energy is Oprah Winfrey, so the rest of us hopefuls—no matter where we stand on the ladder of enlightenment—can only dream of attaining Her level of perfection and keep working like dogs to improve our attitudes.

Nevertheless, there is a slightly irritating and unsettling corollary to the genuine racism horror. The mere existence of this corollary testifies to the very seriousness of racial tension in our world in the first place, and the extent to which, in seeking to combat this baneful reality, human beings can sometimes go off the rails and meander down tangled and rather circuitous pathways. There are, after all, unscrupulous people out there who make money by keeping certain sectors of society at cross-purposes, people who have a lucrative financial stake in human division and chaos—they are the bone-pickers and carrion birds of our day.

ENTER: The Person Who Sees Racism in A Bowl of Cheerios.

Think, too, for a moment, of the Salem witch hunts, when communities were so stirred-up by hatred and fear of the unknown that they started seeing (or concocting) danger when it wasn't even there to begin with, thus churning the overall panic and mania from a fury to a full-blown tempest. I believe that Salem is a good example of what can go terribly wrong when human beings do not "dialogue" in rational ways involving linear (not circular) logic, and when they allow emotion and passion to dictate the way they seek solutions to very real social ills. Salem's plight was about racism, too, if we look very carefully. At the very least, it was about the assertion of unmerited power in oppressive, unjust ways against those perceived to be less than human, less than worthy.

Witch hunt crazes, however, are not the answer to any problem, then or now, and when political correctness is taken to extremes (like anything else in this world) everyone is the poorer for it, and civilization not only begins to fail, but the oppression can turn into a terrifying mirror-image of the same sort of oppression everyone was trying to defeat in the first place!

Dialogue, people.

Let's begin to talk to each other like adults, instead of victims guarding our Victim-acreage. Let us use good humor and common sense to repair what can be repaired, or else remain at war with each other, if that's what everyone wants. If, however, another conclusion is possible, if another epiphany can be experienced, then those who choose to remain at war, no matter which side they are on, or upon which supposed middle-ground they find themselves—those who spurn any attempt to actively heal the wounds and breach divisions make of themselves a more colossal part of the problem, even if their methods are mistaken or unintentional.

Facilitators of injustice come in many forms, just like the Blessed Virgin, who can appear in a vast assortment of food products. It's worth considering.

The All-Inclusive Police Person (Who Doesn't Include Everyone)

—⁂—

THIS COMMENTS SECTION HABITUÉ IS another common example of anonymous internet wildlife and seems to be closely related to Kumbayuh Kathy, if indeed they are not already roommates, or even the same person with two different Disqus accounts. They could well be tinkering with each other's medicinal dosages on different days of the week, too.

Either way, both the All-Inclusive Police-Person and Kumbayuh Kathy reserve for themselves snotty little self-appointed roles akin to those of the hall monitors you couldn't wait to stuff into garbage cans in high school, back in the days when bullying was practically a hallowed institution, instead of a crime worthy of being lethally injected with word-chemicals by Seething Special Snowflakes.

All-Inclusive Police Person relishes his or her role as referee because he or she hasn't got anything interesting or pertinent or even antagonistic to add to whatever comments section free-for-all is taking place, and trust me, there's always a free-for-all taking place. In comments sections, the natives are perpetually restless and the monkeys are forever rattling the bars of their cages.

Just as the drama reaches its zenith (or its nadir, depending upon how you view comments sections in the first place) the All-Inclusive Police-Person will emerge from the cyber-shadows like the unnamed character in some B-Grade post-apocalyptic film wherein the dozen-or-so people who have so far survived the zombies (or malevolent aliens, or cyborgs, or genetically resurrected dinosaurs) are bickering among themselves, and are in danger of attracting unwanted attention from the monsters, and who need a good slapping-down.

—⁂—

SophiesPrimeCut: Why don't you all take a deep breath and release the anger? No opinions will be stifled, here! Everyone is encouraged to contribute and expel the bubbles of uncertainty that plague their systems. Most of you are unable to process a vast diversity of opinions, and that's OKAY. But allow someone who has the power to handle these matters lead you in the right direction. This doesn't happen every day online. Lucky for you I had to call in sick with a headache I thought was stress-related, but which was actually my Ethereal Angel-Self leading me to reach out to you impoverished peons.

—⁂—

As you can see, All-Inclusive Police-Person is, *de facto*, an annoying presence in comments sections, even to people who epitomize "annoying" and who appear to pride themselves upon being human irritants. He or she is probably gunning for a moderator's job, if the favored comments section even has moderators. [EXCURSUS: Just who *are* comments section moderators, anyhow? What DMV test in Hell does one have to fail to get *that* job?] and you can be sure that All-Inclusive Police-Person is angling at least for a PM (private message) from a mod (moderator) saying:

MelvinBubbles: Hey, @SophiesPrimeCut … lately I've noticed what a great job you're doing with the herd, keeping things in line. I'm going to give you a gold star and mention you to the other moderators. We're going to keep our eyes on you."

The All-Inclusive Police-Person will live on that "prop" for a year, even if another tidbit never comes along, and we all know it.

The Snacking Attacker

—ɯ—

LIKE THE AFOREMENTIONED HERDS OF gnu, mowing-down endless acres of savannah scrub as they loiter in the desolate places of the world, one gets the sense that certain species of internet Idiots are likewise eating or chewing something whilst they languish and linger in the comments sections, their yellowed t-shirts exuding pungent odors in the armpit and manboob sections—odors that would force any self-respecting gnu or wildebeest to immediately "up" its musk-game. Their eyes are dull, with lids like storm-savaged Miami canopies, as flies and all sorts of other thirsty little insects flit about the rivulets of viscous fluid leaking onto the puffy, discolored flesh-flaps beneath their eyeballs. Their misshapen faces are cast in a cold, pasty blue aura emanating from the computer screen into the darkened Chamber of their Discontent, moving like some ghoulish klieg light signaling the premiere of a fourth-rate movie-of-the-week starring Liza Minnelli and a three-legged chihuahua in Hell's Version of the Lifetime Channel (which might already *be* Hell—wheels within wheels, friends.)

In light like this, the bag of Doritos at the Snacking Attacker's side is luminescent, the crumbs on the abdomen accentuating the distended beer belly like so many bedazzled rhinestones, the orange-stained fingers practically glowing with power and purpose as they make their way upward to the agog and somewhat drooling mouth, where they shall be licked slowly and with the olfactory appreciation of a prized truffle-sniffing pig. This all takes place before the Snacking Attacker sends those same, moistened and gleaming fingertips to the keyboard where they shall bang-out astonishing gems of acute social observation:

—∾—

KaYBurtonHudson: What the hells a truffle? You think your funny? Whats wrong with a doritoe.? At least doritoes is Murican, unlike you. Your probly a negro from France. One things for sure YOUR A IDIOT!"

—∾—

The 21 Year-Old Illiterate News-Copy Zombie

—ɯ—

THESE DAYS, ONE GETS THE sense that people are bypassing actual news articles and gleaning their information about the world (concerning any given event or matter) via swift perusal of the reactionary bullshit found in the internet comments sections. Yeah, they're going straight to the comments, and a lot of them are brazen enough to admit doing it.

In case anyone is not aware of the weaknesses inherent in this technique, this is worse than the blind leading the blind, because, these days, the *actual* blind have a plethora of navigational methods and reliable means of reading shared data.

As many of this work's readers may have ascertained, I would absolutely trust a blind person to lead me, if I were similarly sightless, before I would allow a comments section dweller to do the same. As many smarter people over the centuries have gleaned, however, the Stupid leading the Stupid is much, much worse.

If, as Christ was said to have remarked, one blind person leading another blind person may cause both to fall, accidentally, into a pit, rest assured that in these days, one Stupid Person will lead another Stupid Person to the edge of the pit, both will gawp at the precipice for a minute, confer with each other in a series of grunting syllables, and then deliberately jump into it.

Because it's there and, well, *adrenaline rush.*

At one time, I would have said that the method of skipping news articles and extracting crucial information straight from the gallery of imbeciles inhabiting comments sections was a dangerous idea. But that was before the rise of another disturbing trend in news copy across all media, one wherein the news copy is as poorly written as are the comments! Therefore, one cannot, in good conscience, blame those who shun actual articles and dive straight into the comments miasma.

When did this horror of horrors begin?

A friend who used to work as a prominent writer for various television series in Los Angeles lamented the state of affairs in which quality writers have, over the past decade and a half, been replaced by drop-outs, dilettantes and skeezy graduates from "creative writing" programs held in someone's garage on weekends and advertised on Craigslist. It doesn't seem difficult to pin-down the source of that "slap in the face of talent" that has been reverberating across the culture for fifteen years. What *is* difficult is avoiding all traces of these increasingly insipid, vulgar, vain, inane, and putrescent "reality" programs intended to reduce the collective popular consciousness to a state similar to that experienced by a human brain infested with dozens of parasitic tapeworms.

My retired Hollywood friend told me that The Powers That Be are apparently now hiring tepid, cookie-cutter 21 year-olds and paying them the peanuts they so richly deserve to compose dialogue for strumpets whose "real lives" are apparently void of anything that even approaches the level of catchy insipidity laid out for them in their given scripts!

The same applies to the world of cinema, where auteurs big and small (I weep for you, Spielberg) are struggling to find funding and the art-form is being demolished. Broadway, the recording industry, you name it.

Standards have plunged along with IQs because no one needs to think in linear terms, anymore. The Lazy Have Been Unleashed! Swift as molasses they cogitate!

Analytical thought? Who needs it? Your phone will get you from Point A to Point B without requiring you to actually understand why you're going from one place to another. We get it. The preponderance of the evidence, save for the exceptions of artistic radiance that stick-out increasingly across the otherwise barren landscape, is incontrovertible. One has to wonder if the same cabal of nitwits and rank amateurs has infiltrated the world of journalism.

Wait. You *don't* have to wonder. They're here.

Once upon a time, editorial standards, even in a provincial news outlet, were upheld with an assiduous sense of pride that stemmed from a combination of quality training, experience, and a consistent—if not unimpeachable—work ethic. Not anymore, at least not in "more" places.

I started to notice the bracing stupidity that had crept like a ravenous melanoma throughout online journalism about ten years ago. News—no matter the subject—appeared to have been documented by nine year-olds hopped-up on Ritalin or else by individuals who wrote their articles in Mandarin and then attempted to run the work through some syntax-butchering online translator, just for fun. It all made one wonder if, indeed, even more jobs had been shipped overseas, and if some poor adolescent on the dusky outskirts of Beijing was being forced to compose accounts of the Mars Rover landings for American consumption.

Deadlines! Deadlines!

Then, I realized: No, it's the same thing that's been happening in Hollywood.

They're simply hiring shitty people and paying them accordingly so that the Big Boys can keep more of the money.

This, my friends, is a method they learned from corporate America, where, for every hardscrabble sales-person fighting in the actual trenches, there are now twelve individuals hired to pick their noses while thinking of new ways to effectively "manage" the people who are killing themselves to pay upper management's unmerited salaries to begin with! It is *insane*.

So, go straight to the comments sections for your meat-and-potatoes info, my friends. Forget about trying to discern much from online articles, where you'll encounter more typos and bits of grating syntax than in a first-edition copy of *Fifty Shades of Grey*. You'll also read uproarious and illuminating things like this:

CINDY CRAWFORD REVEALS HER LIFE BEFORE A SUPERSTAR CAREER IN YODELING

Fox News published a sub-headline like this in 2014, for about ten minutes (before those dipshits corrected it), and I caught it and just about fell off my chair and rolled into the street and crawled into a graveyard and dug-up corpses and turned into a bird and flew over to Big Sur and transformed myself into a crusty fisherman and joined a passing Soviet freighter as a potato-peeler BECAUSE IT WAS JUST TOO FOX!

It exemplified everything monumentally lazy about our so-called media and yet everything tantalizing, too.

I mean, Cindy Crawford is no has-been, and she is *not* some cheap bit of flotsam and jetsam from another era. The woman is legendary, in her field.

But imagine her, if you will, as a woman who did not Model … but as a woman who did, in fact Yodel.

Entire dynamics and paradigms would have hinged in unstoppable ways upon such egregious newsroom errors in the days when one could not "correct" a worldwide-published error in minutes!

Cindy … sweeping across the Matterhorn. Wearing a bikini.

"The Hills are alive …"

Whether Cindy knows it or not, I have a screen-capture of that foolishness and I'm waiting to give it to her in person.

But only in Niedersachsen. During Oktoberfest.

I want to see if she really missed her calling and Fox was trying to both quickly expose and subsequently cover-up a major piece of pop-cultural ephemera.

It may not sound like Cindy Crawford, but it sounds a helluva lot like Fox.

The Great Geek War Of Game Vs. Lore

—⚉—

PREFERRED CYBER HABITAT: Any comments section wherein people can seriously discuss the chances of Galadriel defeating Super Mario with or without the Light of Earendil.

GOOD GRAVY, I LOVE OUR gamers and lore geeks to pieces and you should, too, Gracious Reader! Take a few moments from your humdrum life one day and get to know these fascinating people. Where does one find these lovelies, you ask? Why, any fan-site comments section wherein the comparison of "power levels" can be discussed to the death or at least to the point of a psychotic break is the equivalent of a bustling pub for this marvelous milieu. Another great place to find them (and their comments) is on You Tube channels that feature video clips of "battles" being waged between things that are real (tarantula vs. dung-beetle, mongoose vs. cobra, bumbling tourist vs. gang of drunken bikers, etc.) or between things that are completely unreal and/or ludicrous (Legolas the Elf vs. Ironfoot the Dwarf, Batman vs. Spiderman, Godzilla vs. Any of the Kardashians).

I myself have, on occasion, jumped into the fray on You Tube (of all places) and defended the honor of Tolkien's elf-witch, Galadriel, from those who would dare question her ability to defeat the Shadow of Mordor:

—⚉—

ASSORTED LESSER TOLKIEN NERDS: "Galadriel could never have beaten Sauron. It makes no sense, yap yap yap, etc."

JONATHAN KIERAN: … I don't know if my entire message came across, but, yes, it makes every bit of sense. Re-read the original message. Wash. Rinse. Repeat, if necessary. No one is saying that Tolkien's Galadriel character could have tackled the Sauron character when he was fully empowered, but there's PLENTY of info in Tolkien's body of writings to indicate that she was absolutely one of Sauron's greatest enemies, that she did indeed have the power to repel him in his "not quite fully Ring-y" mode (watch her Magic Mist repel Sauron's Magic Mist during the March of Eorl's army—HA!), and her person was more than a match for his person, so long as he was in a vulnerable state … That's the whole story: a mere hobbit took him down, with the help of great luck, love, wisdom, wizardry, and some starlight in an elvish bottle, along the way … Please reckon with the totality of the story. Tolkien could rarely bring himself to empower female characters, but when he did, they were mighty. Galadriel could have made mincemeat out of a disembodied, reduced Sauron and had time to clean herself up, fix dinner for herself and her hubby, and kick back with a drink in the same evening. Deal with it.

—m—

Seriously, it *does* get that ridiculous when geeks go at it, but come on, we all have a deep-seated, primordial fascination with one-on-one fights between creatures that possess anything resembling teeth. Unquestionably, even in the days of the primeval ooze, in the very thick of the archaic soup where life was first beginning to form and realize it could move about and have carnal relations with other bits of microscopic slop, you KNOW there were virtual coliseums filled with organisms cheering-on a messy dust-up between a strand of prokaryote and a glob of eukaryote. Imagine the heated discussions in the preternatural stands:

"Well, the prokaryote has an advantage due to the gangling cilia, but we must take into account the damage that can be done if the eukaryote begins to expand its plasma membrane, and that's not even taking into account what might happen if the flagellum comes into play!"

Yeah, right. Don't hold me to the protoplasmic science of all that, my beloved geeks. This is parody, after all.

Anyhow, fast forward several hundred million years and you'll discover that the almost lurid fascination with Who Can Beat Who and Why is even more fine-tuned. In comments sections across the planet this genre has reached the status of pseudo-scholarship, if not quite an art form. We have our nerds to thank for all of this rich, nougaty goodness, as well as more conventional blockheads who survived enough ass-kickings in high school to suppress the otherwise telltale nerd-gene all the way back into the shadowy recesses of the id. These latter folk are the good people who talk about boxing, NASCAR, the WWE, old ninja movies, and MME confrontations. Nerds in redneck clothing, if you will. Nerds in camouflage.

God bless them all.

Why? Because we need people like the camo-nerds to go to war and just be able to lunge straight ahead for the sheer thrill of the kill instead of stopping to wonder whether or not they might possess enough "power points" to overcome the shrieking mob of berserkers running toward them with scimitars.

But nerds and half-nerds and pseudo-nerds and nerds-in-the-closet, and anyone with a mere drop of real nerd-blood, really, will rise to the challenge of debating the finer points of a battle between imaginary and long-extinct beings of varying levels of strength.

This is to say nothing of the types who like to spend their days putting sand scorpions into buckets with hungry desert rats and waiting to see which comes out of the ensuing fray with the most appendages intact or at least able to still move with the parts that haven't been eaten or paralyzed. When nerds take these kinds of discussions and bicker incessantly in comments sections over the minutiae, letting the cyber-spittle really fly when it comes to making a case for a *solipugida's* ability to defeat an *atrax robustus* under such-and-such conditions, we call them Geeks. When other individuals do the very same things to the point of having conniption fits, suffering apoplexy, or experiencing heart palpitations in the pages of peer-reviewed publications, we call them Scientists.

But make no mistake: they are both the same species. There is often a great deal of circumstantial overlap. You see, scientists are just nerds with a diploma (or three) and a bit of funding that didn't come from parents watching *Wheel of Fortune* in the living room above the basement, directly over their frustrated heads.

That being noted, it must be stated with all solemnity that society needs its nerds and its scientists to elucidate these deep, pressing matters, because if they didn't, Steven Spielberg would never have existed, the Hollywood blockbuster would never have come into being, and Malibu would be just another stretch of beach, pockmarked with ice-plant, seagulls and happy little gophers, instead of ass-implanted, phony-faced celebrities and their gargantuan palaces sucking the life out of the delicate environment they lecture the rest of us about maintaining.

Trust me, everything meaningful in the universe comes back to nerds debating power-levels, eventually. Quantum Theory is probably involved, but that's just a corollary issue, at best.

Whence comes this gregarious preoccupation with power? Well, it usually begins in nerd-youth, typically involving action-figures, which are NOT dolls, if you are a boy nerd. At least, they didn't *used* to be dolls, not unless you wanted to be as unpopular in your own home as you were in the classroom. One admits that this state of affairs may have undergone a radical change in recent years. Perhaps nowadays the ultra-sensitive couples who spawn nerd-lings actually encourage their children to reject the "action figure" label.

—m—

LITTLE JAKEY: "Mom, can I bring my Transformers action figure to Joseph's birthday party?"

JAKEY'S MOM: "Wait just a minute, there, Jakey. The word 'action' implies aggression, and we wouldn't want to bruise or invade another child's safe-space with a forceful vocabulary, would we?"

LITTLE JAKEY: "Um … no?"

JAKEY'S MOM: "Good boy. So when you get to the party, make sure to let everyone know it's a sissy-doll."

—m—

Who knows? Today's devoted parents probably do say things like that and more power to them, because that will save untold millions of nerd-fated children from any number of complexes and neuroses. Even so, rest assured that the fun begins with the toys—plastic dinosaurs, in my day—and then works its way up through the brain-frazzling acceleration of video games, Ninja Turtles, Transformers, Etch-A-Sketch and other things. If multiple-fanged or magically endowed characters of any kind can be thrown into an impromptu skirmish, nerds will do so, and subsequently dissect and analyze the proceedings and possibilities with feverish enthusiasm.

That is precisely why we love them.

Rhonda The Reasonable (Who Starts Out Reasonable And Then Loses Her Goob By The End Of A Comments Section Battle)

—◊—

YEAH, SHE STARTS AS MILD as milquetoast, seemingly full of wisdom and replete with thought-provoking adages that sometimes even soften the hearts (if not the already pulverized and murky minds) of the beasts and trolls.

Rhonda appears to be the beacon of balanced, heartfelt diplomacy—not too dispassionate, not too earnest—as she unravels her pseudo-motherly voodoo upon the quacking, chittering, cursing buffoons.

The comments world pauses to admire the emergence of a soul so rare and vital as to present sane ideas with the tender determination of a cherished schoolmistress or parochial-era nun, one of the few that didn't use a ruler to rap knuckles into bloody stumps.

A hush may even come over the comments section for a moment, denoting the dozens of invisible blithering idiots now stunned into pervasive self-reflection by Rhonda's near-Socratic grasp of the human dilemma and how it pertains to the ongoing argument about the proliferation of cuckolded men in Western society.

Tears are shed onto keyboards and keypads, mixing with the encrusted chunks of Frito and Cheetoh residue that have thwarted SHIFT and RETURN keys for weeks. Deep thoughts of epiphanic magnitude are experienced in the wake of Rhonda's wisdom, as the aforementioned tear/Cheetoh mix becomes a swampy paste falling in clumps to the bottom of the keyboard, there to commune with the flecks of dead skin, streaks of body oil, errant pubic hair, and vast colonies of microscopic dust-mites.

Rhonda has stilled the tempest and yet she has stirred the waters. She has calmed the rabid and unsettled denizens of the cyber-rainforest with the illusory sentience of her worldview. A moment of human harmony has been experienced ... like a star over some lonely manger in the Middle East.

Then, Rhonda ruins the whole goddamned spell by opening her trap like a crazed banshee in the comments section, reveling in the sheer magnitude of the power she has wielded. This Sorceress of Social Media, drunk with the almost sexual satisfaction of the thrall in which she has imprisoned her cowed minions, tilts her head back, gloats in her own glory, swigs another mouthful of cheap Chardonnay, and proceeds to type something utterly ... revealing:

—❡—

RHONDABELLE: Screw all this illusion and doom. I'm sick of being a mediator! I want to scratch my face until I bleed and bark at the moon while the rest of you swirl around the cultural toilet bowl like floaters in the waterpark of Hell's 8th Cesspit!"

—❡—

I can't tell you, Gracious Readers, how many times I have seen these Reasonable Rhondas fall from grace and, in the midst of their fateful nose-dive toward the jagged terrain of their doom, end-up revealing all of the perversions they had been trying so hard to keep under wraps.

RHONDABELLE: I started out with such innocence. I only wanted a better world. What happened to me?

GorgoPoo: WE happened. Did you really think you were going to escape the grip of our devastating little gremlin-fingers?

RHONDABELLE: Away with you, dour spirits! I call upon Fellini, I call upon Giulietta Masina, I call upon Marcelo Mastroianni, I call upo

GorgoPoo: Thats right. Pass out, Rhonda. The battle is already lost, whether you were right or wrong.

Even so, do not feel too much grief for Rhonda. True, she will retreat like a scorned animal, scuttling in shame from her keypad like a maimed spider. She'll crawl into bed, pull the covers over her head with intermittent swigs from her leaking bottle. She will gnash her teeth a bit and rue the fact that she lost control once again—AGAIN!—after she had them all eating out of the palm of her hand, and then she'll fall into a dark and fitful sleep. This is a sleep filled with nightmares of clowns handing out blue balloons shaped like revolvers and ice cream cones filled with centipedes. Come the dawn, however, Rhonda will awaken and shake off the previous night's sheen of flop-sweat, renewed and determined to recapture her comments section glory.

There is always another comments section to stalk, always another chance to prove her mettle. After all, her name is not really "Rhonda" and she'll never meet any of the people she's trying so desperately to deceive … including herself.

The Tinfoil Milliner

—◊◊◊—

THESE ARE THE FOLKS WHO will give you six teeth-grinding, sphincter-contracting polygraph essays which detail the plot on the part of a secret cabal of mind-controlling warlocks trapped in a pyramid atop the Washington Monument and their plans to unleash the ebola virus upon society through strategic dispensation via Starbucks brown-sugar packets. These warlocks, of course, are funded by the Koch brothers, who are themselves merely a front for the Illuminati.

Have not we *all* suffered from the delusions of the Tinfoil Milliner in our lives? Our grandparents and great-grandparents suffered thusly, and therefore we must take up the burden of enduring this peculiar form of social oppression even in our day, the Day of the Comments Section. Behold—the arrival of the internet comments section was, for the Tinfoil Milliner Community, as glorious a watershed moment as was the evolution of *Chiroptera* to the rabies virus, when that baneful disease hitched a ride upon the first bat in the primordial mists of time.

Today, Tinfoil Milliners of every description and delusion have the chance to create awkward moments in worldwide settings instead of being abruptly abandoned at the edges of countless bars near a wheezing Pac-Man game, exiled to the Kids' Table at holiday meals, or forced to build their own dates in Mommy's basement out of Crisco cans, pink flamingo pool floats and a couple of rusted Slinkys. In these days of more nuanced and technologically diverse ways to "bring the crazy," the Tinfoil Milliner has indeed been able to refine his art-form. He has sunk his arm to the elbow in the more amply stuffed grab-bag of paranoiac possibilities from which to choose on the internets. He has supped heartily upon the veritable smorgasbord of selling-points for the suspicious-minded.

It used to be extraterrestrials and the Kennedy assassination, mostly, but today's Tinfoil Milliner has evolved. If he has not quite learned how to blend-in seamlessly with the other comments section mutants, he has at least managed to expand his repertoire. You'll never be surprised to find him lurking in your favorite comment section, but some of you who are mothers will be astonished to learn that he is, in fact, hard at work in your own basements. He is bathed this very minute in a sheen of perspiration after experiencing yet another Eureka-moment in which the Illuminati's newest diabolical ruse to infiltrate the magically protective aluminum force-field has been discovered, and millions of Milliners around the globe—connected by the stalwart brotherhood of the internets—must rise-up as one and alert the unenlightened.

Bring him some milk and cookies, Mom, before you even bother to go down into the cellar and see all of this for yourself. I guarantee you he's going to be hungry and he's going to be up all night.

The "Get Rich Like My Clinically Depressed Sister Just Did!" Entrepreneur

—◊—

THESE DELIGHTFUL PEOPLE ARE VERY much like those suction-headed remora fishes that are forever hitching a ride beneath the jaws of sharks and irritating the hell out of them.

"Wait!" you say. "The remora, though annoying, performs a valuable service to the shark by clearing away various parasites and catching errant pieces of mutilated fish-flesh and other tasty bits of gore that escape the shark's maw during a feeding frenzy."

Right, and that's exactly what the Get Rich Quick Entrepreneurs will say to you when challenged by the dozens of commenters they annoy with their intrusive and random posts in your favorite comments section.

"We are performing a valuable service to commenters by momentarily distracting them from the various parasites that infest the forum. We also assist by catching errant pieces of human failure and other inconsequential bits of social detritus. As an added bonus, we offer people the illusion that they can perform valuable services while wearing three-day-dirty pajamas at home and getting paid corporate CEO-caliber wages for their efforts!"

Yeah—that's what such people would say … if they bothered to stay around comments sections long enough to actually hawk their wares with a little more razzle-dazzle than a thirsty, cobbled-together bit of claptrap like:

TerrySuccess: "WOW! I thought my family was doomed to repeat generational welfare but everything changed when my sister, Jennifer, discovered a way to make $7,000 a month without ever leaving her own kitchen, her incapacitated & emphysematic husband, Geary, and her bipolar mother who occupies the shed out back! And she did it in one simple, secret way that will BLOW YOUR MIND!"

Bojingles: Shit. It's late. I'm drunk. Broke. My bipolar Mama lives in the attic, so I guess we have something in common. Can you tell me the secret without the need to follow your link, cuz I don't think I can take that right now.

It's little wonder that seven out of ten internet commenters surveyed find the Get Rich Entrepreneur more irritating than trying to remove an eyelash blocking one's vision while driving a car, only, try as you might, you just can't get hold of the damned thing and it keeps dangling before your pupil like some sort of freakin' ghost-hair until you finally snarl a bit and start tugging at *all* of your eyelashes because there's no way that single, unhinged lash can survive if you pull hard at *all* of them, right? And then, after nearly running over a kid on a bike and careening through a stop-sign you get hold of yourself, look down at your palm in terror and find seven perfectly healthy and formerly fully attached eyelashes in your hand *BUT THE GHOST-LASH IS STILL IN FRONT OF YOUR EYEBALL!!!*

That's the level of annoying that most surveyed commenters ascribe to the Get Rich Quick Entrepreneur, but don't take my word for it. Results of these highly scientific surveys are found throughout the media and the internets. Just like the entrepreneurs who proliferate in comment sections with their tantalizing come-ons.

—⁂—

LisetteBushwack: I answered one of those ads and ended-up collecting Alpaca-feces in Hemet, CA, to process and then create fuel for synthetic motocross races between David MisCavidge and Tom Cruise. It doesn't seem so far-fetched, when you start-out working for gods. Then you get bitten or infected from the Alpaca droppings and things change. They change …

—⁂—

People in comments sections usually ignore such "Get Rich" posts, much like a Great White appears to be utterly oblivious to the dachshund-sized freeloader sucking a 60-mile hickey into its skin. Occasionally, however, some resentful denizen will note the incongruous interloper who has no business interrupting a discussion about ass-implants with an incongruous business post, and will flag the Get Rich Quick Entrepreneur. Others will try to crack a quick joke, typically along the lines of wondering if so-and-so's mother or sister made "all that money" on the living room floor in the comfort of her own home, or something similarly bilious and common. Yeah, welcome to the charm of the internet.

I, however, have more often wondered about the people in comment sections who actually follow the Get Rich Quick Entrepreneur's links and find themselves sucked into a never-ending vortex of intrigue and organized criminal mischief. I ponder the webwork of ruin that requires all the espionage powers of the CIA, FBI, and INTERPOL to save Stupid

People from some Nigerian witch-doctor's cage, into which they have been sequestered for fattening before ultimate dissection (while alive) and the removal of vital organs.

Because we all know that's *exactly* what happens to people who answer those ads in comment sections.

The Yelp Whelp ... And Other Commenters Who Comment Upon Comments

—◆—

PART OF THE RAGING CLUSTERFUCK that has come with giving every sociopathic misanthrope an easy opportunity to render ill-considered opinions about anything and everything is that enough brainless shit-heels can actually damage someone's otherwise respectable and thriving small business by posting a shallow and reactionary "review" on Yelp. Because human beings are such groupthink sheeple and mob-mannered creatures, one illiterate review brings out the illiteracy in two or three more yap-flapping goofballs who see Jimmy-Swain's erudite critique and apparently say to themselves,

"Hey! That guy is as dumb as me, and I been in that store before, too. I could write somethin' as stupid as him and I'm havin' a bad day, anyhow, so why not HOGPILE?!!"

This is the disgraceful underbelly of human nature, and we all goddamned know it. In this current polarized social atmosphere, wherein people who have nothing substantial to say about anything are encouraged to "take sides" and form dimwitted alliances pitting Team This against Team Whatever, the phenomenon is especially disheartening.

In the olden days (1994–"cough") people who wanted to render a staunch opinion in a public forum had to actually *think* of one, then sit down, pick up a pen, compose and maybe even type an actual letter requiring the complex interaction of verbs, nouns, prepositions, punctuation marks, adjectives, and occasional adverbs known as a "sentence." After exerting brain power to transfer the whole thing into a statement that one (quite self-consciously) hoped others would deem coherent and worthy of consideration, the opinion was mailed to a newspaper, or onward to the upper management of a company that needed, in one's opinion, to know about certain deficiencies meriting swift attention and correction. People invested time, effort and solemnity when it came to public complaints because, in the human realm, value and quality used to be the byproducts of time, effort, and solemnity.

Well, kiss that shit goodbye!

Our era is now one wherein concepts like time and effort have been exiled to the sidelines like so many wheezing hindrances on the race-track to personal fulfillment. Careful deliberation is often seen as something that stands in the way of an illusory "authenticity" that comes with split-second immediacy in the thrall of our virtual reality. Western culture is paying a steep price.

Why?

Because the split-second thoughts, opinions, and first-impressions of most brain-baked human beings in this new millennium are rarely "authentic," objective, substantial, or worth sharing with their pets, much less the entire world!

In other words, most immediate human thoughts are fit only for the cranial garbage disposal that our species has evolved specifically for the purpose of trashing and recycling insignificant reactions, inappropriate emanations, fleeting emotions and other elements of mental flatulence. Nowadays, however, everyone has done away with the filter, as if the mental filter (like

Time and Effort) was an oppressive slave-master. Once human beings melded soul and mind to instantaneous technological facilitation, there was less need (or incentive) to brush aside the steady stream of mental eructations that everyone experiences during the course of any given day. There is less interest in picking and choosing one's public expressions as the brain receives and processes sights, sounds, smells and sensations of every sort, preserving and highlighting the Necessary and eliminating the Trivial—or what ought to be trivial. What we are left with in this society, under such circumstances, is ... well, the Trivialization of Everything.

Matters have degenerated to such a state that thousands feel no compunction whatsoever when it comes to unleashing swift opinions no more weighty than brain-farts and, sometimes, by adhering to a total "sheeple pattern" of behavior, in which one idiot strikes a chord with several other idiots (who are never in short supply) reality is not *documented* by immediacy—it is instead skewed and distorted. In these cases, objectivity flies out the window with every other sign of sentience, rationality, and good character. The sad part is that someone's livelihood can be irreparably harmed in this atmosphere of rampant triviality.

—⁓—

NimNuk: I so totally really totally wanted to like this little wine-tasting room, but, when I got there, I was so so so so wasted from the twelve other tasting rooms me and my friends had visited, that I realized I'd left my purse with the bubbly-wine people down the street and my panties at the Pinot place! LOLZ! Anyhow, these people wouldn't let us in to taste, saying we were late or most of our shoes were missing, which when they say that to good customers like us ALWAYS means their wine is BAD BAD BAD!!! And I should know, because I've tasted bad wine at many places that wouldn't let me in. Objective reviews are very impertinent to me."

NimNuk: Oops! I meant to say "important." BURP. lolz

—◆—

Yelp, my ass. Even in places like Amazon and You Tube, "reviewers" are encouraged to over-discuss the comments about the comments about the comments in any given section. What a vortex! What a discordant symphony of stupidity! Once upon a time, people had to handle "comments" on their own two feet, not hiding behind an anonymous internet username. It's all swirling 'round the bowl, friends, and believe me when I say that it will degenerate to the point wherein the front yard of every neighborhood home and apartment-building hallway will be one day be outfitted with digital information-screens that prominently broadcast for fellow residents, passersby, and the satellite cameras of Google Earth how those dwelling within are being rated by their spouses, children, and roommates on any given day:

—◆—

212 OAKTREE LANE: I found my husband, Lee, drunk and passed out with his head in a Black Widow's web on the *lanai* last night. And me working 60 hrs. a week. Do U Think this is symbolic?

2237 DOVETAIL DRIVE: Casey refused me for the 12th consecutive time and there were 9 dirty dishes in the sink when I got up to make coffee. Anyone interested in assisting?

107 PECKERWOOD CIRCLE: Everyone on this cul-de-sac thinks that Donald is a paragon of virtue and that I am a viper in the grass, but I have SEEN his browsing history and he favors pornographic sites featuring grown women and Little People with leaf-blowers.

7920 PALMETTO LANE: The children I've bragged about for years both failed their final exams. Betty's kids, next door, whom I have often likened to scrawny & soulless praying mantids, passed their tests. NO peach cobbler for us this evening!

72 BUTTERFIELD COURT: The Mormons who stopped by yesterday did not taste as good as the Mormons who knocked on my door a month ago. I understand when fast-food companies skimp on ingredients, but when actual religions start throwing quality-control to the wind, there's something wrong. Anyway: Jehovah's Witnesses welcomed today, ALL DAY. Knock around the backyard basement door. Bring plenty of pamphlets.

—⊸—

The Jehovah's Witless

—⚬—

THESE CARD-CARRYING ALUMNI OF THE University of Smug are perhaps an offshoot of the same evolutionary tree that sprouted the Big Word Hurlers. I refer to this one as a "Jehovah's Witless," however, because the magnitude of his or her humorlessness approaches the level of divinity. The Witless are nonetheless an especially entertaining sideshow in comments sections across the multimedia spectrum, if only due to that glaring deficiency of wit they display while attempting (and failing) to produce anything that even remotely approaches Gravitational Pull on the Planet Clever.

Of interest to note is that the Witless are usually the very first ones in a comment section who make it a point to launch flaming attacks upon someone who *has* managed to pull-off a reasonably clever remark and, in their covetousness, these comedically challenged souls lash-out like trembling, neurotic little ferret-people. Yes, they seethe with envy and grumble on the sidelines because they are forced to watch a bigger, smarter, faster predator gnaw leisurely upon a carcass of satire they would never be able to tackle on the best day in their most incandescently moist dream.

Why are the Witless like this?

Well, first of all, they know, deep down in their chemically self-loathing cerebral cortexes, that they are dreary, anemic buzz-kills with the comedic skills of an avian flu bacterium, and yet there's nothing they want *more* in their greedy, groping souls than to be considered "funny," or, at the very least, "amusing." What makes this a drama of Gothic proportions is that they know, with all the certainty of taxes and death, **THAT THEY NEVER WILL BE FUNNY.** (Hey, one can go "All Caps" to maximize someone *else's* idiocy, too.)

This realization is not quite enough to kill the Witless, but it *is* enough to send them into paroxysms of jealousy and nostril-flaring rage when they see anyone else entertain a crowd online. This is like a crucifix being brandished before the eyes of the vampirically un-gifted, who nevertheless fancy themselves to be *repartees* and *raconteurs*, but who, in real life, have endured or created UNTOLD BLUSH-WORTHY MOMENTS OF CRICKET-INDUCING AWKWARDNESS at parties. These are the people who confect horrid moments at soirees—moments for which they've practiced their sassy little comments for weeks before the fete, in front of mirrors, in different tones of voice, with variating hand-gestures, all so they can hear the approving sound of a chuckle or two. Then, when the moment arrives to tell their anecdote (or render their online comment) they squat like clumsy, flightless birds and lay one enormous, stinking egg, meeting with reactions that range from uncomfortable silence, half-hearted smiles and, if lucky, a couple of stilted sympathy-giggles. On the part of the unimpressed audience, there follows a quick glance around the room to look for people capable of holding proper court and, always—*always*—a mass-exodus in furtive steps away from the Witless One. Yes, The Witless One is left alone to contemplate a dreary shrimp canapé and suffer burning sensations in the swamp of his armpit regions, wondering where it all went wrong.

Worst of all, the Witless don't know a thing about damage control. They continue to stand, hoisted on their own petards, *right in front of that goddamned hors d'oeuvre table!* Yes, they do. They stand there and clutch their wine-glasses with pale, glowering faces that make them look like marbled Grecian monuments to the horrors of Irritable Bowel Syndrome. Yes, they stand there and actively despise the rest of the world for its failure to appreciate the talent they know all too well that *they* lack!

Dear friends, if you've read this far in my book you're either witty (in which case, call me up and we'll go out for drinks), masochistic, or abjectly stupid. Even if you're genuinely witty only in your brain, that counts. Truly it does. You don't have to be a performer.

But we all know that not everyone can be clever in the same way that not everyone can be physically attractive, or rich. Or intelligent. Comments sections are like oracles in terms of revealing this fundamental truth.

Wit is a subcategory of intelligence and being rich may buy you a certain amount of laughter at a party because you're paying for the booze and the hookers, but no amount of money can buy you hilarity, so the laughs are fake. Still, the rich don't care as much about that, which is one of the blessings of money. Ask any bald, white, 55 year-old guy with a micropenis driving a Ferrari and who is currently in escrow on a house in the Hamptons. He pays *himself* to believe he's always the funniest guy in the room, and it works.

But the genuinely Witless are manifesting just one more of the many forms and disguises of the Green-Eyed Monster. They are, to the very last, jealous and bitter creatures, desperate to have something they want more than anything else in the world, and that "something" is, for them, unattainable.

You either have it or you don't when it comes to wit, kids. Thus, these Witless wastes continue to unload their baleful, uninteresting neuroses in comment sections, where they know they can't be so conspicuously abandoned near the Chardonnay ice-bucket and the wheel of brie imploding into a musky dusk like their social lives. Sadly, even in comments sections, these also-rans will lash-out like distempered cats at those who are truly funny.

—m—

JOrdiWig: So I told these people, 'Why don't you leave before someone drops a house on you, too?' It split that party wide open!

Amphitrite: @JOrdiWig By half the people leaving due to such a worn-out line, I expect, you dimwit.

JOrdiWig: @Amphitrite May your meat-flaps wither and rot, dropping from your fetid thighs to scorch the earth with your wickedness, you H8R!!!!!

Amphitrite: Whull, if you'd been that quick last night I guess the entire party wouldn't have died like the Masque of The Red Death, eh?

—m—

What alternative do they have, these Witless hordes? In the throes of their desperation, the Witless hit rock-bottom by forming little societies comprised solely of those guaranteed to always be as witless as they are … and then they proceed to bore each other into catatonia in a glorious cavalcade of astonishing mediocrity.

The Witless sometimes call these societies "salons."

We call them "The Breitbart Comments Section." But that is an entirely different book.

The Grammar Fuehrer

—⁂—

THERE COULD BE A MAJOR debate about the presence of those affectionately called "Grammar Nazis" in comments sections, but I prefer to throw a red-herring onto the dusty path by identifying these people as Grammar Fuehrers.

Yeah, yeah—these bastards tend to police comments sections like so many goose-stepping acolytes of Goebbels and Goehring, but I'd like to make a case for allowing a bit of latitude to the Grammar Fuehrers.

I get it: even if we all admire intelligent specimens, no one likes a brazen know-it-all, and in the end you have to ask yourself, "What's worse? A snotty show-off berating and correcting commenters for every little grammatical infraction … or the insufferably stupid who clog comment threads like so many globules of stroke-inducing plaque in the arteries of human discourse?"

Yes, you know and I know that you ask yourself that very question all the time, and I also know what your secret answer is.

You pick the Grammar Fuehrer.

Unless you have the communicative skills of a Cro-Magnon hunter who has suffered irreparable brain-trauma following a mastodon attack, there is really no other answer, at least not for the intelligent.

But sitting in your comfy chair, your hot-tub, a jail cell, or wherever else you might be reading this book, it's not so easy to decide in favor of the Grammar Fuehrer, so I would like to steer the uncertain among you toward the value of context in this delicate matter.

A Grammar Fuehrer is indeed one of those repellent souls obsessed with drawing attention to the errors of others, no matter how minuscule, in order to boost a self-esteem that otherwise could barely sustain the sputtering pilot-light in the rank stovetops of their self-loathing psyches. Hardcore Grammar Fuehrers contribute nothing to any comments section in a thematic or topical sense—they are simply there to whip people about the fingers with a baton and humiliate them with reptilian deliberation.

I, for one, do not believe that this sort of critique has any automatic relevance, especially if a commenter—though not quite as educated as one might hope—is attempting to convey a salient point. Worse, it is obvious that the Grammar Fuehrer is seeking to demean by employing the smokescreen of higher learning. I'm with most of the inevitably hog-piling commenters on this one:

"Shut up, Grammar Fuhrer! Nein! We will not tolerate your facetious tirades in these unhallowed halls! Achtung!"

This, or something similar, is usually enough to send the Grammar Fuehrer back to its fetid bunker. But even though there is something deplorable and repugnant about correcting someone's grammar while interrupting a dialogue (of any kind) just for the sake of self-congratulatory jollies, not *all* online grammar correction is a bad thing, people.

Look around you.

The standards of human discourse are receding faster than the hairlines of any number of current Hollywood blockbuster stars that keep the lace-front wig-moguls in business. Take a look at any comments section with more than twenty posts, anywhere. Across the globe. Literacy levels are *down*. Do you want your Special Snowflake Children to one day distinguish themselves like this:

—⚊—

Jess569: Graduate today was like the end but the first some was the MOST my mom & dad got me a CAR Mursaydees-====o hell i was REDDY for everything we are JUMPING JUMPING JUMPING!!!! I take filosofee in the Fall. This party aint even startet

—⚊—

I didn't think so.

There may well be those who counter by saying, "Wait a cotton-pickin' minnut! You said it weren't rite 4 the smarty pantz people 2 correct the stoopid one's."

That's mostly true, and I stand by it, but there are cases wherein a little neighborly correction ought to be considered a radiant beam of altruism rather than a blatant attack.

Give at least some well-intentioned Grammar Fuehrers a break, people! Take a few deep breaths and remember those trusty little pointers for next time. You'll be glad you did. Not a single one of us is perfect. Sadly, all of us merit correction and critique throughout our mayfly existences. Hopefully we'll be assisted at opportune and ideal times, but life doesn't work that way. If you receive helpful advice in a good-natured manner, consider yourself … well, *helped*. As much as we must necessarily loathe the obsessive and oppressive Grammar Fuehrer, we must be quick to excoriate the trolls who exude particularly horrific grammar.

Seriously, if your spelling stinks but you're trying to make a coherent contribution, you deserve to be left alone, unmolested. If you're a sociopath moron with deserved literacy issues and your sole aim is to insult people, you need to spend some quality time with Grammar Fuehrer. Ask him for his number.

Remember: in the comments section, we are all neighbors, if we are anything at all.

Any Divorced Guy In A Trailer At Midnight

—⟋⟋⟍—

HE'S NOT READY TO HIT the bars ... not yet.

It's only been a few hours since the ink on the divorce papers managed to dry, and he's been banned from Shorty's, Stinky's, and FudPucker's, already.

The local Hooters has his name and face on a sepia "outlaw wanted" poster tacked prominently at the combination stripping-pole/hostess-stand just inside the door.

Even the haggard gal who runs The Cherry Pit-Stop has issued a lifetime G-string excommunication upon him with all the solemnity of an infallible pontiff closing the gates of heaven to some brazen heretic who threatens to lead the vulnerable flock toward the infernal Cesspits of Perdition.

But he is not a heretic. Nor is he an outlaw. He is ... a divorced guy in a trailer at midnight, and he's going to contribute to the comments section discourse, damn it, if it's the last thing he ever does. He's not proud, he's desperate, and for that reason he'll frequent places where you'd least expect to find him.

No matter where you find him, however, be prepared to read him and weep.

—ɯ—

HARLEY DENTON: I don't know why i come here to this forum every night. There's hardly anyone ever here and i dont even know what aromatherapy is. But the people I've met seem so nice and I can't drive to Stumpy's, what with my license revoked. The taxis wont come to this park after sunset either so here i am again on a Saturday night lol.

Sienna Windsong: Hey Harley, I'm here! Glad to see you back. You should really read the FAQ about our forum and the benefits of aromatherapy. I think it could really really help you at this critical juncture in your life. Really.

HARLEY DENTON: Hi Sienna! Thanks. I'll read that shit tomorrow. Promise. Right now I just need to connect with another human being. Do you want to PM me?

Sienna Windsong: Now Harley, you KNOW what I told you the last time I went into private message mode with you. I'm not falling for that again. I have nothing against free sexual expression, but some of the things you said were really really offensive. I know it came from a place of loneliness, but …

HARLEY DENTON: Yes, I am very lonely. Very. It's like a black sort of lake filled with tar in the center of my heart. So was it the bathtub with ice cubes that put you off? cuz I can talk about other stuff besides that. I swear. Got a million ideas.

Sienna Windsong: Well, the bathtub thing was definitely out of line but the bit about the motorized, rotating chimney-sweep machine was what really tipped it.

HARLEY DENTON: Oh. I've had some trouble with that before online. It must be the way I describe things. I'm so clumsy with words Sienna. If only i was as good with words as I was with other parts of me I would probably not turn off so many beautiful and loving ladies. lolz.

Sienna Windsong: Look, I'm really rooting for you and sending positive emanations. I know the divorce from Tina was very traumatic.

HARLEY DENTON: Her name was Tiny. Not Tina. Tiny.

Sienna Windsong: Right. Anyhow, I'm on your side and trying to provide a welcome atmosphere for you, here at the *Making Scents Out of Heartbreak* discussion board, even though you have shown absolutely no interest whatsoever in aromatherapy or its incredible healing powers, and you pretty much sexually harassed me when I agreed to PM you the other night. But we're about acceptance, here, Harley, and I want you to know that I hope you find your true and definitive Self, the one waiting for you at the other side of this bleak horizon, dancing in the light of dawn's first redeeming rays.

HARLEY DENTON: Thank you, Sienna. I want to dance in those rays so bad i can taste it. It's sweet. And I can picture it, too. Naked. Dancing in the rays. You know, I knew you were a angel the first time I saw your name on this board. Windsong, I said. Thats a name that the angels would use. And i was right.

Sienna Windsong: Sweet of you to say so, Harley. If only you would let me send you the recipe for my lavender, sandalwood and Tea Tree oil blend, I know it could be a centering force in your otherwise dismal existence.

HARLEY DENTON: Lavender, sandalwood and Tea Tree oil. Would that make a good lube for intimate moments?

Sienna Windsong: Good night, Harley. And *namaste.*

—⚒—

The Agitated Codger

—∞—

HE MIGHT BE CONSERVATIVE. HE might be liberal. He might be anywhere in-between. But in any given comments section, several things are always certain about The Agitated Codger.

1. He fought and survived some war at some (perhaps unspecified) period of time.
2. He has *never* failed to pay his taxes (Goddamn it!)
3. He raised his family in a time of great strife and they all turned out brilliantly. (This is a most dubious claim and the Codger himself may be in absolute denial or living at such a distance that he doesn't realize his children are, in fact, drug-addled fools, so he must therefore be forgiven.)
4. The current state of human civilization has never been worse.
5. Modern youth have no respect for anything.
6. He doesn't need Viagra like some poor, pathetic fellow codgers because he has been a non-stop Love Machine since his youth and only people of ill-repute require the assistance of "them jump start flagpole-raisin' tablets!"
7. He never thought he'd see the day when "this" would happen in the world (and "this" can always mean a whole lot of "that.")
8. He never before stooped to such a low thing as commenting in an internet comments section, but felt that—just this once—it was his responsibility to communicate his abject disgust after reading the

article about Bruce Jenner's transition from Olympic legend and reality-show star into Caitlyn Jenner—Olympic legend and reality show star in a come-hither bustier.

9. He is always (or almost always) a "He." Older women don't seem to experience an inordinate amount of internet agitation, or, if they do, they tend to conceal it brilliantly and allow any agitation to manifest itself in acts of insurrection against the codgers who dwell in their homes via things like arsenic and hiding the TV remote. This is most appropriate.

Whatever the motivation, I, for one, can never argue about the value of all our Agitated Codgers the world over, wherever they may be. If you live in a nation that has actually won some wars, take a moment and thank your local codger when you see him, keeping in mind, of course, that they are almost always agitated. Even so, that doesn't mean they won't appreciate your efforts.

—⚏—

NostraDumbAss: All American flags should be burned as relics of a bygone age signaling the horrors of nationalism and the doom that awaits all who would pledge their allegiance to a murderous federation led by a cabal of jackbooted jingoists!

JaZAMM: Speak that Truth to Power, comrade!

VJDAYEdgar96: I'll tell you what, you ungrateful little no good limp wristed commie liberal spoiled brat ME Generation millennial tree hugging Democrat Obama-voting welfare-sucking lily-livered chickenshit PUNKS! You better thank your lucky stars that men like me were around to fight for your right to spout this kind of treasonous nonsense in these United States because I'd hate for the life of me to see what might've happened if YOU had been called to serve your country back in the day. We'd all be wearing kimonos and licking each other's eyeballs for fun if this great nation had been in your hands!

NostraDumbAss: Oh go exfoliate your dead skin cells @VJDAYEdgar96 because I'm about to puke from the old man smell rising like a toxic cloud of stank from your post.

JaZAMM: LOL!!!!

NostraDumbAss: You selfish bastards are gonna regr

VJDAYEdgar96: WTF is that supposed to mean?

JaZAMM: We're waiting.

NostraDumbAss: Whoah …

JaZAMM: IKR? I think that old man keeled right onto his keyboard!

NostraDumbAss: Totally! We bagged ourselves an Agitated Codger! This is historic!

JaZAMM: Awesome! Look, dude, I gotta go. My mom wants me to take out the recyclables.

NostraDumbAss: L8R.

—⚎—

Then again, you might just end a war hero's life if you can't display some common online courtesy. Remember, chances are you owe your very "freedom to comment" about celebrity sex scandals and sundry to an Agitated Codger, not to some whiz-kid from Silicon Valley. So get a grip on yourself, your keypad, your sense of respect and make some gall-danged room for any and every codger you might encounter online, while those codgers are still blessedly among us.

The Puppy Suckler

—⚍—

This is, by far, my favorite comments section denizen of them all. This is the one person who, in the midst of an enthusiastic, ongoing comments section debate or discussion, suddenly admits (without a trace of irony or inhibition) to some sort of personal behavior that is worthy of immediate 51/50 hold or a quick visit from concerned members of Children's Protective Services. The Puppy Suckler can also be that commenter who, in the diaphanous thrall of morally relativist thinking and the throes of a high-kicking Rockette fugue-state, actually tries to wrap their brains around *another* commenter's twisted, warped deeds and "understand" their point of view, even to the point of mounting a vigorous defense, at times.

I have in fact encountered the Puppy Suckler in all her glory and here is a transcript of her Magnificence:

—⚍—

jennyquark55: Bummer. Just saw in the news that our local zoo had to euthanize a baby platypus because its mother refused to feed it.

ElAmandaSquee: @jennyqurk55 That's just bullshit. They could've found someone willing to suckle it.

jennyquark55: A baby platypus?

ElAmandaSquee: Why not? I mean, my Rottweiler, Maisy, had a gland infection a few years back and I suckled all of her pups myself. It was awesome.

jennyquark55: You WTF?! You don't mean your own breasts?!

ElAmandaSquee: Of course with my own breasts! What else? The puppies turned out so well that I suckled Maisy's next three litters. Or I helped, I should say.

PoNash: @ElAmandaSquee Whoah! Did I just read this thread right? You breast-fed your dog's puppies?

ShaLina19: Now before y'all start to judge, I'm a dog-lover and, while I never suckled a puppy, I would do a lot for my Trixie if she had a chronic female problem. Just saying

ElAmandaSquee: Wait a minute @ShaLina19, my Maisy didn't have gland problems but just the once. I suckled the subsequent litters because it was a powerful spiritual experience.

jennyquark55: OMG! Are you insane, lady? Why didn't you get formula and those little eye-droppers from your vet? That's what most people do in those situations!

ElAmandaSquee: Maybe, but most people are not aware of the pleasures to be found in inter-species bonding practices. That's their problem.

PoNash: Damn. I hope you ain't got kids.

ElAmandaSquee: As a matter of fact I do. I have a son, and he was breast-fed right alongside Maisy's puppies. It's the most beautiful sensation in the world to nourish hungry mouths of all kinds.

ShaLina19: Hell, even *I* can't behind this shit. I'm outta here ~~~~~>

ElAmandaSquee: You're all just haters. It's no surprise that narrow-minded people like you could never grasp the wonder of two different species sharing the energy of Life.

PoNash: Hold on, I'm not a H8er. I could maybe grasp it. It'd help if you could send me some pics.

jennyquark55: @ElAmandaSquee @PoNash You're both disgusting

ElAmandaSquee: @jennyquark55 Why can't you open your soul and embrace the planet's diversity? Can you honestly sit there and tell me that if one of your beloved pets was in need of intimacy and physical nourishment, and you were the only one who could give it, that you would refuse that pet?

jennyquark55: Yes, I would refuse it!

ElAmandaSquee: How can you possibly know that for sure?

jennyquark55: Because I raise tarantulas.

—⚡—

Where does one begin? Well, I suppose it's worth mentioning that inter-species suckling has not *always* ended up badly. Look at Romulus and Remus, for Jupiter's sake. The entire Roman Empire was founded upon lupine teat-suckling! That's quite an endorsement. Then again, we all know what eventually happened to the Roman empire, and there might be a lesson there, but it is beyond the scope of this study to determine whether or not the decline and fall of the world's greatest civilization was in any way connected to the dynamic of humans weaned on wolf-milk. That is for other scientists and historians to explore. Not I.

In the midst of conundrums like this, I try to think about Betty White and Doris Day. Those two Golden Era superstars and admirable ladies have done and—at least at the time of this writing—continue to do a heck of a lot for animals. Still, I shudder to think of either one of those gals suckling a puppy. I think, in fact, that Betty White should serve as a healthy and reasonable barometer in this delicate matter.

I have a feeling that Betty White would be firmly against it. Not so sure about Doris, but I have a hunch that saucy old Betty would blanch at the suggestion. If, on the other hand, Betty White would have no compunction whatsoever about drawing a thirsty cur to her bosom and at least attempting to proffer nourishment, then I say we may want to rethink the mainstream viability of this practice. If Betty White would endorse this behavior, if she would gladly and willingly give suck to a canine, then let it be.

Come, all ye Rottweilers, Labradoodles and Shih-Tzus! Drink at the fulsome oasis! Gather, ye Bloodhounds, Chihuahuas, and Mastiffs—feast heartily at the paps of plenty!

Would Betty White suckle a puppy? That is the question you should ask yourself in the deep, dark, loneliness of the night. Go ahead. Ask and tremble at your conclusions.

* Now that I think about it, though, using Betty White as a yardstick of rational judgment may no longer merit the credibility of which it once could boast. She did, after all, spend six seasons attached to *Hot in Cleveland*. This alone raises serious questions about her faculties and sense of propriety.

The Ineffably Lonely

—◊◊◊—

AFTER ALL OF THIS INCISIVE, painstaking, oh-so-scientifically re-searched—and hopefully amusing—exploration of the wonderful world of Anonymous Internet Commenters and the panorama of creatures, great and small, who inhabit such places, there is only one more observation to make regarding the possible motivations, the reasons, why so many millions are finding solace and a sense of community in the phenomenon of comments sections.

Yes, there is a less than admirable impetus behind the human desire to contribute to the Great Cacophony, but I think there is another, very fundamental reason, one that perhaps all of us should be a bit more aware of, when it comes to ways in which we interact with the fellow dwellers on this big blue ball hurtling through space toward an ultimately unknown and often existentially terrifying destination.

People are lonely.

As mentioned, and as millions now realize, the more meaningful aspects of human discourse are being increasingly devalued and trivialized. After all is said and done, most of us truly do crave substantial and meaningful human companionship. Spare a thought for the Agitated Codger, the Puppy Suckler, the Big Word Hurler, and the Guy Who Reads His Bible on the Toilet, all of whom may be attempting to camouflage their inner-pain and loneliness with an outer shell of lewdness, aggression, disrespect, hysteria, and wanton eccentricity.

Choose compassion when possible, Ye Commenters, because, chances are, if you're frequenting a comments section, there's a lonely little candle fluttering in the soft pink boudoir of *your* hungry heart, too.

Don't let anyone snuff it out.

And if you don't buy into any of this "people are simply lonely" bullshit, well, just sit back and enjoy the show, because *every* night is going to be a bumpy night in the comments section. You might even get to discuss how a proper Heavenly Miracle Contest is supposed to end …

The Amazing Adventures Of God ... Cont'd

—⟋⟋⟋—

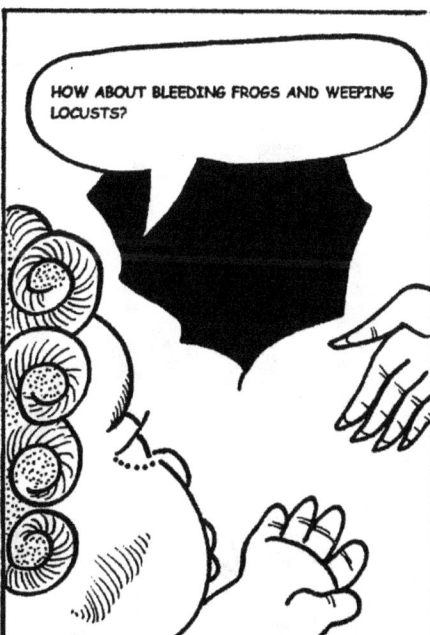

www.ingramcontent.com/pod-product-compliance
Lightning Source LLC
Chambersburg PA
CBHW050119280326
41933CB00010B/1159